What Was African American Literature?

The W. E. B. Du Bois Lectures

WHAT WAS
AFRICAN AMERICAN
LITERATURE?

Kenneth W. Warren

HARVARD UNIVERSITY PRESS

Cambridge, Massachusetts, and London, England

2011

Printed in the United States of America

Library of Congress Cataloging-in-Publication Data

Warren, Kenneth W. (Kenneth Wayne)
What was African American literature? / Kenneth W. Warren.
p.   cm.
Includes bibliographical references and index.
ISBN 978-0-674-04922-2 (alk. paper)
1. American literature—African American authors—History and criticism—
Theory, etc.   2. African Americans in literature.   I. Title.
PS153.N5W348   2010
810.9'896073—dc22   2010015714

In memoriam
Autry L. Warren
Nora Frances Warren

Contents

ACKNOWLEDGMENTS

My thanks to Henry Louis Gates Jr. and to the W. E. B. Du Bois Institute for the opportunity to give the 2007 W. E. B. Du Bois Lectures, which form the basis for this book. A portion of Chapter 2 was delivered as "W. E. B. Du Bois's *Dusk of Dawn: The End of a Beginning in African Americanist Inquiry*" at the Hart Institute at Pomona College as part of its 2002–2003 Lecture Series "Public Intellectuals/Public Issues." I'm also indebted to the participants in the American Cultures Workshop at the University of Chicago for helpful responses to portions of the text. And as always, thanks to Maria.

WHAT WAS AFRICAN AMERICAN LITERATURE?

I

HISTORICIZING AFRICAN AMERICAN LITERATURE

Historically speaking, the collective enterprise we now know as African American or black literature is of rather recent vintage. In fact, the wine may be newer than generally acknowledged, which is to say that it was neither pressed on the African continent nor bottled during the slave era. Rather, African American literature was a postemancipation phenomenon that gained its coherence as an undertaking in the social world defined by the system of Jim Crow segregation, which ensued after the nation's retreat from Reconstruction. This social order, created by local and statewide laws, statutes, and policies, received constitutional sanction in 1896 with the U.S. Supreme Court's decision in *Plessy v. Ferguson* and was maintained for decades by violence and intimidation, buttressed not only by the work of scholars, scientists, artists, and writers but also by the quotidian social practices of ordinary citizens. Yet it was through many of these same means that this order was challenged and sometimes acquiesced in by its victims until it was finally dismantled, at least judicially and legally, in the 1950s and 1960s. African American literature took shape in the context of this challenge to the enforcement and justification of racial subordination and exploitation represented by Jim Crow. Accordingly, it will be my argument here that with the legal demise of Jim Crow, the coherence of African American literature has been correspondingly, if sometimes imperceptibly, eroded as well.

Admittedly, my insistence on this rather constricted historical frame for something called African American literature may seem at the very least counterintuitive and at the most simply wrongheaded. Indeed, much recent literary criticism and scholarship has sought to justify taking a longer historical view of African American literary practice. Some have argued that African American literary texts are distinguished by the way black authors, consciously and unconsciously, have worked and reworked rhetorical practices, myths, folklore, and traditions that derive from the African continent. Others have maintained that African American literary texts are defined by a prolonged engagement with the problem of slavery, a system of labor exploitation that was central to the development of not only the United States but the whole of the Western world. Those making the latter claim have held that writing against or under the influence of the slave regime has defined not only the literature written prior to abolition but also subsequent black literary practice, because black literary practice as a whole has been indelibly marked by the ways that enslaved blacks coped with the brutalities of the Middle Passage, when millions of Africans were transported from Africa to the Americas, and chattel slavery.[1]

Also arguing against the view I am taking here is that individuals of African descent certainly wrote during the period before the historical advent of Jim Crow America and have continued to do so, in ever increasing numbers in the years since the dismantling of de jure segregation some forty-five years ago. Why should the works of Phillis Wheatley, Jupiter Hammon, Frederick Douglass, and so many others written during the antebellum period not count as African American literature? And what of the undeniable fact that African Americans continue to write what they understand to be African American literature? To insist that African American literature "was" is to raise the question of what all of this ongoing production "is."

The last of these objections might have been met more easily had I given this book the title *What Was Negro Literature?* For it is undeniable that while most, if perhaps not all, of the writers who published work during the Jim Crow era understood themselves to be *Negro* writers—publishing, sometimes willingly, sometimes unwillingly, Negro literature—no (or at least very few) contemporary writers of African descent describe themselves as writers of Negro or colored literature, preferring instead black or African American—a difference that reflects broad and significant social and political changes. Indeed when contemporary writers do allow themselves to indulge a fondness for earlier nomenclature, they tend to do so nostalgically, reproachfully, or perhaps in a manner combining both moods. One example is a brief exchange in Andrea Lee's episodic 1984 novel *Sarah Phillips* where, upon hearing the white girlfriend of the title character's brother urge him to "do a black history project on your family," the narrator's elderly Cousin Polly objects, saying, "I don't like that word 'black.' . . . Colored folks used to think that word was an insult!" Of course, embedded within Cousin Polly's objection is her disapproval not only of the word itself but of the interracial relationship she is being presented with, and the paradox that only in a world where "black" and "African American" prevail as favored terms will the genteel sons and daughters of the colored elite be able routinely to consider, even if only to reject, the possibility of marrying "outside" the race. For a character whose "southern voice" has already prompted the novel's eponymous heroine to describe the old woman as "a living fossil, one of the Paleozoic creatures that are periodically discovered in deep waters," it will clearly not avail to learn that "black" is not an insult but merely "what kids are saying now."[2]

Yet, however small the number of people at the present moment who share the full measure of Cousin Polly's distaste for the word "black" (or her association of the term with interracialism), her belief that the bygone era when we were all colored (to paraphrase the titles of two mid-1990s memoirs by, respectively, Henry Louis Gates Jr. and Clifton Taulbert) may still surpass the post–Jim Crow world in terms of nurturing a sense of group cohesiveness and pride has found ready affirmation among a variety of critics and writers.[3] And though this nostalgic yearning rarely crystallizes as an injunction to rehabilitate this older terminology, it does coalesce in a concern that the baby of racial unity is in danger of being thrown out with the bathwater of segregation just at that moment when such unity is presumed to be as necessary as ever.

That these changes in preferred nomenclature, from "colored" and "Negro" to "black" and "African American," can be correlated, however imperfectly, with the political and legal dismantling of Jim Crow does raise the question of whether or not these shifts marked more than a shift in terminology.[4] My contention is that to a great extent something significant has changed. Yet my decision not to use "Negro" literature in my title was determined by a sense that African American writers and critics of the postsegregation era have often remained oriented by the project of Negro literature as it was defined by responses to Jim Crow—partly as a result of the above-mentioned nostalgia, but more fundamentally as a consequence of believing that, in some crucial ways, Jim Crow has not ended and that in "the aftermath of the civil rights movement, the most obvious expressions of segregation and discrimination gave way to more covert but equally pernicious manifestations of racism."[5] My objection to this point, which will be elaborated upon more fully as this argument unfolds, is not that racism has disappeared from the nation's sociopolitical landscape, but that pointing out the persistence of racism is not to make a particularly profound social observation or to engage in trenchant political analysis. Rather, I think it important to see that a political and social analysis centered on demonstrating that current inequalities are simply more subtle attempts to reestablish the terms of racial hierarchy that existed for much of the twentieth century misunderstands both the nature of the previous regime and the defining elements of the current one. By glancing at a few relatively recent texts, I hope to show that this previous orientation can no longer provide coherence for a contemporary African Americanist literary project. As Danielle Allen has argued, the period between the *Brown v. Board of Education* decision in 1954 and the passage of the Voting Rights Act in 1965 constituted an "epochal shift in the country's history . . . [that] remain[s] still undigested."[6]

As for the status of the fiction, poetry, and letters written before the Jim Crow era, my claim is that the mere existence of literary texts does not necessarily indicate the existence of a literature. James Weldon Johnson's introduction to Sterling Brown's 1932 collection of poetry, *Southern Road,* expresses a view along the lines I'm tracing here. Johnson writes,

> The record of the Negro's efforts in literature goes back a long way, covering a period of more than a century and a half, but it is only within the past ten years that America as a whole has been made consciously aware of the Negro as a literary artist. It is only within that brief time that Negro writers have ceased to be regarded as isolated cases of exceptional, perhaps accidental ability, and have gained group recognition. It is only within these few years that the arbiters of American letters have begun to assay the work of these writers by the general literary standards and accord it such appraisal as it might merit.[7]

Although Johnson's words provide plenty to quibble with, including (for my purposes) the exactness of his chronology, his observation helpfully distinguishes between the existence of writers from an ascriptive group (even writers whose merit is broadly acclaimed) and the conceptualization of works by multiple authors from this group as *a literature*. The former does not depend on the latter. In Johnson's brief comments, 1920s black writers such as Brown, Langston Hughes, and Claude McKay were writers of Negro (African American) literature, while figures such as Phillis Wheatley or Frederick Douglass had been simply Negroes who were writers—or perhaps one could helpfully say that they were writers who were *not yet* Negro writers and that antebellum writing by black Americans became African American literature only retroactively.[8] I'll add here that while I think my claim in regard to antebellum black writing is correct, my argument does not stand on making it categorical. That is, I would be willing to concede in the face of textual evidence that some black writing before the Civil War was understood by its practitioners and readers as something like a distinct literature, but I would still insist that whatever this literature was, it was changed significantly by the necessity of confronting the constraints of the segregation era. Indeed, it was largely in the light of imperatives determined by the Jim Crow era that antebellum texts were assimilated into the collective project we recognize as African American literature.

Of course, this being said, it bears observing that the transformation of "not yet *x*" writers into the status of ancestors and progenitors of more recent authors is a prerequisite for establishing any national literature, a fact that, in turn, raises the question of whether or not the observations I am making here significantly distinguish African American literature from other literatures. By way of providing an answer, I'll turn briefly to a core insight in Erich Auerbach's *Literary Language and Its Public,* which has been suggestive in helping me articulate my sense that African American literature might be viewed as a "historical" entity rather than as the ongoing expression of a distinct people. Writing in the late 1950s, Auerbach asserted,

> European civilization is approaching the term of its existence; its history as a distinct entity would seem to be at an end, for already it is beginning to be engulfed in another, more comprehensive unity. Today, however, European civilization is still a living reality within the range of our perception. Consequently . . . we must today attempt to form a lucid and coherent picture of this civilization and its unity.[9]

With some significant qualifications, I am arguing here that, mutatis mutandis, African American literature as a distinct entity would seem to be at an end, and that the turn to diasporic, transatlantic, global, and other frames indicates a dim awareness that the boundary creating this distinctiveness has eroded.

What I'm interested in pursuing here is not Auerbach's "method" of attending to the historical processes, institutional effects, and social pressures as these broader forces are reflected in and refracted through authorial style. Rather, I'm more interested in Auerbach's insights that these contextual forces shape a shared set of assumptions about what ought to be represented and that as these contexts themselves undergo change, those representational and rhetorical strategies that at their peak served to enable authors and critics to disclose various

8

"truths" about their society can begin to atrophy and become conventionalized so that they no longer enable literary texts to come to terms with social change but operate instead as practices of evasion. Along this line, my argument is that African American literature is not a transhistorical entity within which the kinds of changes described here have occurred but that African American literature itself constitutes a representational and rhetorical strategy within the domain of a literary practice responsive to conditions that, by and large, no longer obtain.

From this standpoint, recent claims that either distinctly African traditions or the experiences of slavery and the Middle Passage constitute the center of African American imaginative and expressive practice should be seen as symptoms of the breakdown of a former coherence. The "public" of African American literature was the public, both black and white, defined by the assumptions and practices of the segregation era. Whether African American writers of the segregation era acquiesced in or kicked against the label, they knew what was at stake in accepting or contesting their identification as Negro writers. By contrast, the entailments of being regarded or not being regarded as an African American writer at the present moment are comparatively less clear. My argument presumes, then, that African American literature can be treated as a historical designation that exhibits both the precision and the fuzziness accompanying all period labels. Of course, any insistence on historical periodization is justified only if it leads to interpretive clarity. My contention here is that this periodization can aid our interpretive efforts by drawing attention to some of the factors that almost unavoidably oriented African American literary practice during the Jim Crow era. Specifically, black writers knew that their work would in all likelihood be evaluated instrumentally, in terms of whether or not it could be added to the arsenal of arguments, achievements, and propositions needed to attack the justifications for, and counteract the effects of, Jim Crow. As James Weldon Johnson observed in 1928, "I judge there is not a single Negro writer who is not, at least secondarily, impelled by the desire to make his work have some effect on the white world for the good of his race."[10] Writers also knew that their work would likely be viewed as constituting an index of racial progress, integrity, or ability. Added to this was the paradox that the success of black literature as a political tool threatened to undermine its status as an index of black integrity. The pressure exerted by these instrumental or indexical expectations shows up not only in the way that writers and critics regard African American literary texts but also within the works themselves.

To paint in somewhat broad strokes, "The After-Thought" to W. E. B. Du Bois's *The Souls of Black Folk,* in which Du Bois pleads that his "book fall not still-born into the world-wilderness," exemplifies an "instrumental" understanding of his own book as having been written to achieve a social end.[11] On the other hand, Du Bois expresses an "indexical" view of African American literary writing when he puts forward the "Sorrow Songs" as evidence of the inner nature and capacity of the Negro race, or when he writes in "The Negro in Literature and Art" (1913) that the "time has not yet come for the development of

American Negro literature" because "economic stress is too great and the racial persecution too bitter to allow the leisure and the poise for which literature calls."[12] To expect literature to serve as an indictment of this economic stress and racial opinion is to make an instrumental demand on literary practice; to expect African American writers to produce great literature once economic stress and persecution wane is to take an indexical view of literature.

That Du Bois approaches literature both instrumentally and "indexically" should make it clear that these two terms cannot produce a neat taxonomy of African American writers, or even African American texts, for that matter. That is, my aim here is not to define one set of writers who can be grouped under the heading "instrumental" and another set under the "indexical" label. Nevertheless, it might be possible to credit a claim that "instrumental" applies better to a writer like Sutton Griggs, who was more likely to treat his fiction as merely another means of achieving the same social ends he pursued through his essays, lectures, sermons, and the like, than it does to someone like Claude McKay, who insists that his racial identity was so inescapably part of his work and the work of all great writers that "a discerning person would become immediately aware that I came from a tropical country and that I was not, either by the grace of God or the desire of man, born white." That is, McKay, despite his political activities, was more inclined to view writing as an end in itself than was Griggs, for whom social and moral ends were always paramount. In describing his approach to his writing, McKay insisted that while his "social sentiments were strong, definite and radical," he nonetheless "kept them separate from [his] esthetic emotions, for the two were different and should not be mixed up."[13] By contrast, such mixing defines Griggs. And yet, even Griggs was not indifferent to the idea of a novel as an art form whose successful execution would redound to the credit of the race as a whole. "Observe that all of the races of mankind that have achieved greatness have developed a literature," Griggs wrote in his book of philosophical and ethical musings, *Life's Demands; or, According to Law*. He continued:

> Not a single race that has no literature is classified as great in
> the eyes of the world. . . .
>
> Where people have not the habit of reading there will not
> be much writing. The future progress of the Negro race calls
> for an awakening on the part of the people to the necessity of
> cultivating the habit of reading and stimulation of the art
> of making literature as indispensable aids to the development
> of the spirit of patriotism.[14]

Here, the instrumental and the indexical intertwine as Griggs combines a hortatory call for blacks to read and write literature with a view of literary achievement as a metric for assessing the progress of the race as a whole. Likewise McKay, despite his insistence to the contrary, did not fully insulate literature from political ends. As every student of the Harlem Renaissance knows, McKay's most famous poem, "If We Must Die," was taken as an eloquent protest against the violence of the Red Summer of 1919, when race riots broke out in cities and towns across the United States, including most prominently, Chicago, Washington, D.C., and Elaine, Arkansas.

The point here is that no writer of this period could operate indifferently either to the expectations that African American literature ought to contribute demonstrably to some social end or to the belief that novels, poems, or plays constituted proxies for the status or the nature of the race as a whole. Writers could, and did, insist that their works be judged without regard to their identities and without reference to the political or social status of the black race, but the mere insistence was an acknowledgment of the pressure of these expectations.

It is also true, however, that calls for writers to do their part in achieving social ends were not indifferent to art's special status as a realm apart. Even Du Bois's well-known claim in "Criteria of Negro Art" that "all Art is propaganda and ever must be, despite the wailing of purists" is not so much a disparagement of the idea that art should be an end in itself as it is an argument that, for the time being, art must serve instrumentally as "propaganda for gaining the right of black folk to love and enjoy." In other words, until society realized the conditions in which black artists could practice art as an end in itself, art would have to bear the burden of serving as a means to an end. The recognition of African American art simply as art would depend on society's achievement of racial equality. Or, as Du Bois writes, once "the ultimate art coming from black folk" is deemed "to be just as beautiful, and beautiful largely in the same ways, as art that comes from white folk, or yellow, or red"—that is, once "the art of the black folk compells [*sic*] recognition, [then black folk] will . . . be rated as human."[15]

Such a view has not fared well in recent decades. Writing in the late 1980s, Henry Louis Gates Jr. remarked on and lamented the role played by indexical and instrumental imperatives in producing black literature. Tracing the problem back to the eighteenth century and Thomas Jefferson's dismissal of Phillis Wheatley's poetry as lacking originality, and therefore as an indication of the inferior status of the race as a whole, Gates writes,

> Unlike almost every other literary tradition, the Afro American literary tradition was generated as a response to eighteenth- and nineteenth-century allegations that persons of African descent did not, and could not, create literature. Philosophers and literary critics, such as Hume, Kant, Jefferson, and Hegel, seemed to decide that the absence or presence of a written literature was the measure of the potential, innate humanity of a race. The African living in Europe or in the New World seems to have felt compelled to create a literature both to demonstrate implicitly that blacks did indeed possess the intellectual ability to create a written art and to indict the several social and economic institutions that delimited the humanity of all black people in Western cultures.[16]

Gates adds, "Few literary traditions have begun or been sustained by such a complex and ironic relation to their criticism: allegations of an absence led directly to a presence, a literature often inextricably bound in a dialogue with its potentially harshest critics." Accordingly, Gates writes, "black criticism, since the early nineteenth century, seems in retrospect to have thought of itself as essentially just one more front of the race's war against racism," which meant that "an author tended to be judged on his or her fidelity to 'the Black Experience.'" Gates describes this conception of critical practice as "a dead end for black literary studies."[17]

As I hope is clear to my reader by now, my claim is that had African American literature not been viewed "as essentially just one more front of the race's war against racism," it would not have existed as a literature. So although Gates is right in noting that racist assumptions did mar much criticism of black literature, his complaint conflates levels of observation that were better kept separate. For example, it is important to recognize that Jefferson's reprehensible criticism of Wheatley did not stem from an expectation on his part that distinct races ought to produce distinct literatures. Rather, he was decrying what he believed to be the absence of any worthy achievement by blacks in the literary and creative arts. In the same section of *Notes on the State of Virginia* in which he disparages Wheatley, Jefferson also faults Ignatius Sancho, whom he ranks as the more accomplished of the two but still places at "the bottom of the column" of literary achievement for failing to evince the "sober reasoning" appropriate to his subject.[18] The norms championed by Jefferson, while applied invidiously, are not norms that align specific peoples with specific literary sensibilities. The alleged shortcomings of black writers as noted by Jefferson, and the response of black writers throughout the eighteenth and first half of the nineteenth centuries to charges of black intellectual inferiority, were not expressed as a failure to achieve *a* literature but rather as a failure to achieve *in* literature. The literary societies that Elizabeth McHenry describes as proliferating among free blacks in the antebellum north were not workshops for the production of a distinct black literature but salons for producing works of literary distinction.[19]

By contrast, the imperative to produce a black literature could not become fully operative until later in the century. It was only subsequent to the abolition of slavery that black and white writers in the U.S. context came collectively to hold the race accountable for producing a literature. Whether writers condemned slavery for the cruelties it visited upon black people or, like Booker T. Washington and (at various points) Sutton Griggs, they credited slavery for having introduced blacks to Christianity and the West, no one could argue that slavery provided the optimal conditions for producing a literature. To be sure, the incorrigible Jefferson in *Notes* compared chattel slavery in North America favorably with Roman slavery during the Augustan era to draw invidious distinctions between the capabilities of blacks and whites. But notwithstanding his conviction that literary genius could overcome the obstacles of enslavement, widespread calls for the production of *a* literature by black Americans did not become standard until late in the nineteenth century.[20] At that point, despite the poverty facing most of the former slaves and the political and social barriers erected against them, emancipation did unleash a host of predictions that, in the wake of abolition, the nation and the world would see what the true capacities of the black race were—an expectation voiced not only by skeptical whites but also by black northern elites intent on proving the worth of black people and constituting themselves as the true representatives of the race.

But there is more at stake here than distinguishing the Jim Crow era from the preceding period. It is also important to place in its appropriate context Gates's desire to extricate African American literature from indexical assessments of racial progress and instrumental responses to systematized second-class citizenship. Problematic for Gates has been the way the "functional and didactic aspects of formal discourse assumed primacy in normative analysis" of literary texts. Lamenting what he describes as a "confusion of realms," Gates observes, "The critic became social reformer, and literature became an instrument for the social and ethical betterment of the black person."[21] The issue here is not a matter of endorsing or dissenting from the idea of black literary critic as social reformer (although, as I've argued elsewhere, that posture at the present moment is often deeply problematic).[22] Rather, I want to argue the irrelevancy of bemoaning or advocating for what Gates sees as inattentiveness to literary matters among black writers and critics. One cannot treat African American literature as a literature apart from the necessary conditions that made it a literature. Absent white suspicions of, or commitment to imposing, black inferiority, African American literature would not have existed as a literature. Writers of African descent would have certainly emerged and written novels, plays, and poems that merited critical attention, but the imperative to produce and to consider their literature as a corporate enterprise would not have obtained. The achievement of black writers lay in their having responded creatively to the imperatives that derived from the establishment of a social order on the basis of assumed black inferiority, and not in any transcendence of these imperatives. Black writers, as both creative writers and critics, to paraphrase Marx, made African American literature, but they did not make it just as they pleased, and certainly not under circumstances chosen by themselves. More importantly, black writers made black literature only and precisely because they encountered circumstances they would not themselves have chosen.

So what were some of the other entailments of writing against and in the shadow of Jim Crow that proved decisive for the development of black literature? One was facing the paradox that the condition one was fighting to overcome was the very condition that gave one's own existence meaning. As an instrument for pursuing social justice, this literature was forced at least to contemplate its own wished-for obsolescence. To some extent, of course, this is the paradox of all reformist or revolutionary movements, but when we consider Du Bois's self-assessment in his "Apology" to his 1940 autobiography, *Dusk of Dawn,* the paradox takes on a specific form. Du Bois writes,

> My life had its significance and its only deep significance because it was part of a Problem; but that problem was, so I continue to think, the central problem of the greatest of the world's greatest democracies and so the Problem of the future world.[23]

The wording here suggests that the deep significance of Du Bois's life hinges less on his contribution to the resolution of the problem than on his being part of a problem that it appears will be around for a long, long time. The sentence's syntax balances the contingency of being a problem in the first clause with the assurance of the problem's persistence in the second. I don't mean at all to imply that Du Bois relished the second-class status of Jim Crow or that he didn't wish and work fervently for its defeat. I do, however, want to draw attention to the way that, for Du Bois and other African American writers, the limitations of the black condition get rewritten as a paradoxically fortunate turn. These writers posit an American ideological machine so powerful in its capacity to change its citizens into soulless automatons that, paradoxically, its most obvious victims turn out to hold within themselves the only hope for its redemption. In the third chapter of *Dusk of Dawn* Du Bois writes, "Had it not been for the race problem early thrust upon me and enveloping me, I should have probably been an unquestioning worshiper at the shrine of the social order and economic development into which I was born."[24]

Or one could paraphrase Du Bois by saying, but for the race problem, he would likely have been a run-of-the-mill, reasonably wealthy white man—an outcome we would be inclined to reckon as a loss given the esteem in which we hold the man that Du Bois did become. And if we harbor any doubts about which path we ought to prefer for Du Bois's career, we can settle the matter by turning to the plot of James Weldon Johnson's 1912 novel, *The Autobiography of an Ex-Colored Man,* a work that can be seen as exploring the road not taken in Du Bois's assessment of his own life. The story of a young man who lives out his early childhood not realizing that according to prevailing social mores he is black, Johnson's novel—which explicitly mentions Du Bois's *The Souls of Black Folk*—attempts to play out Du Bois's cultural program as laid out in both *Souls* and "The Conservation of Races," in which the race's mission is to develop its own message or gift to the world. Accordingly, in the wake of being informed that he is black, Johnson's protagonist believes for a time that the path to heroism, distinction, and service is the path that runs through black identity, which for him entails working up black folk culture into high art that could contribute to the broader cause of racial equality. Unfortunately for his quest, he witnesses a lynching in the south, and the consequent trauma derails him from his ambition, sending him north where he allows himself once again to be taken for white. The fate awaiting him along this alternate route through white identity, however, is undistinguished financial success in Du Bois's "dusty desert of dollars and smartness."[25] This journey, from white identity to black identity and back, is meant to impress on Johnson's readers that his protagonist has lost something almost invaluable in being black no more. Or as Johnson's narrator puts it, when he considers "that small but gallant band of coloured men who are publicly fighting the cause of their race" he sees himself as "small and selfish . . . an ordinarily successful white man who has made a little money."[26] But to grasp the full import of this observation, we must take it a step further: If to live without a sense of racial mission counts as a loss when the race as a whole still faces the challenge of over-

throwing Jim Crow, then might it not be possible that the ultimate overcoming of Jim Crow itself will also be experienced as
a loss as well as a gain? That is, if in Johnson's novel the appeal
of black identity derives significantly from the opportunity
that identity provides for living heroically—the opportunity to
be something more than run-of-the-mill—then will not such
an appeal dissipate once such heroism is no longer demanded?
Is the future as imagined by African American literature to be
understood as a world in which the destiny of black character
is to be, so to speak, run-of-the-mill?

Du Bois attempts to conjure such fears in order to allay them
in "Criteria of Negro Art," an essay that seeks to highlight the
emptiness of American whiteness by hypothetically turning
black people white. That is, after describing the boorish behavior of a group of white "Americans" he encountered while on a
trip to the Scottish border, a land he describes as steeped in the
romance and poetry of his youth, Du Bois asks his listeners:

> If you tonight suddenly should become full-fledged Ameri-
> cans; if your color faded, or the color line here in Chicago was
> miraculously forgotten; suppose, too, you became at the same
> time rich and powerful;—what is it that you would want?
> What would you immediately seek? Would you buy the most
> powerful of motor cars and outrace Cook County? Would you
> buy the most elaborate estate on the North Shore? Would
> you be a Rotarian or a Lion or a What-not of the very last
> degree? Would you wear the most striking clothes, give the
> richest dinners and buy the longest press notices?

Even as you visualize such ideals you know in your hearts that these are not the things you really want. You realize this sooner than the average white American because, pushed aside as we have been in America, there has come to us not only a certain distaste for the tawdry and flamboyant but a vision of what the world could be if it were really a beautiful world.[27]

Although Du Bois presents his answer as if it were axiomatic that, absent racial barriers, blacks would not want to be white, buried not too deeply within his claim is the anxiety that race might be merely skin deep and the difference between black and white aspirations nothing more than a fairy tale told by the black elite to give luster to what are, for the most part, petit bourgeois concerns. The devastatingly realistic portrayal of black Chicago politics in the second section of his 1929 novel, *Dark Princess,* fleshed out Du Bois's apprehension that for those who had gained a modicum of relief from the strictures of Jim Crow, a life defined by buying press notices, giving rich dinners, and the like was indeed the ideal that guided black striving.

In fact, throughout the Jim Crow era, African American writers have sought to build support for a racial project by giving their readers a glimpse of the emptiness, or at least the insufficiency, of dominant white American ideals. For example, Erma Wysong, the heroine of Sutton Griggs's 1901 novel *The Overshadowed,* advises a distressed vernacular-speaking black preacher, "We must learn to quit accepting customs as good and grand, simply because the white people have adopted them."[28] The lesson of Jessie Fauset's *Plum Bun* is that the best that white society has to offer are soul-destroying temptations. Ralph Ellison's review of Gunnar Myrdal's *An American Dilemma: The Negro Problem and Modern Democracy* (1944) chastises Myrdal for concluding, " 'It is to the advantage of American Negroes as individuals and as a group to become assimilated into American culture, to acquire the traits held in esteem by the dominant white Americans.' " By way of demurral, Ellison notes that aside "from implying that Negro culture is also not American," Myrdal's analysis "assumes that Negroes should desire nothing better than what whites consider highest" even though in the "pragmatic sense" lynching and Hollywood, faddism and radio advertising are products of the "higher" culture, and the Negro might ask, "Why, if my culture is pathological, must I exchange it for these?"[29]

Of course, the answer to Ellison's question goes without saying—as it does in a large array of African American texts. For example, the advertisement for the "miracle of a kitchen" that beguiles Lutie Johnson, the ill-fated protagonist of Ann Petry's *The Street* (1946), and leads her to accept a housekeeping job in Connecticut, where she sees firsthand the pathologies of rich white existence, is another example of this gambit. And from Toni Morrison's *The Bluest Eye,* where white baby dolls, movie stars, and spotless kitchens stand for false white ideals, through her *Tar Baby, Song of Solomon,* and *Sula,* in which various characters fall short of becoming who they ought to be, a witting and unwitting capitulation to "white" ideas is the recurrent problem. Morrison, of course, is a post–Jim Crow writer, but I'll address this complication later.

In the meantime, suffice it to say that other instances from within the Jim Crow era abound. Indeed, one telling measure of how appealing it was for writers to contrast the potential richness of black identity with the baseness of white American ideals is the fact that Richard Wright, who was more likely to remark on the "cultural barrenness" and the "essential bleakness of black life in America" than to extol black cultural resources, resorted to this tactic on occasion. In his autobiography *Black Boy (American Hunger),* he recalls that the white waitresses with whom he worked in Chicago often told him of "their tawdry dreams, their simple hopes, their home lives, their fear of feeling anything deeply, their sex problems, their husbands." He continues:

> They were an eager, restless, talkative, ignorant bunch, but casually kind and impersonal for all that. They knew nothing of hate and fear, and strove instinctively to avoid all passion.
>
> I often wondered what they were trying to get out of life, but I never stumbled upon a clue, and I doubt if they themselves had any notion. They lived on the surface of their days; their smiles were surface smiles, and their tears were surface tears. Negroes lived a truer and deeper life than they, but I wished that Negroes, too, could live as thoughtlessly, serenely as they. The girls never talked of their feelings; none of them possessed the insight or the emotional equipment to understand themselves or others. How far apart in culture we stood! All my life I had done nothing but feel and cultivate my feelings; all their lives they had done nothing but strive

for petty goals, the trivial material prizes of American life. We shared a common tongue, but my language was a different language from theirs. . . .

And I was convinced that what they needed to make them complete and grown-up in their living was the inclusion in their personalities of a knowledge of lives such as I lived and suffered containedly.[30]

The resemblance between Wright's observations here and Du Bois's from "Criteria" is striking, down to each author using the same adjective, "tawdry," to describe the goals of white society. For Wright the paradox and pain of having "suffered containedly" is that he, as a figure for all African Americans, has come to possess a depth of experience and complexity of vision clearly superior to the dominant society he is supposed to value and emulate. Within this condemnation is an argument that in order for American society finally to grow up, it would have to learn to speak in the occluded language that it had forced on Wright and those like him.

To see what his white female coworkers see and value is to recognize that theirs is not a kingdom of culture. Rather what comes to the fore is the way that their

(constant outward-looking, their mania for radios, cars, and a thousand other trinkets made them dream and fix their eyes upon the trash of life, made it impossible for them to learn a language which could have taught them to speak of what was in their or others' hearts. The words of their souls were the syllables of popular songs.)

For Wright, then, the "essence of the irony of the plight of the Negro in America, to me, is that he is doomed to live in isolation while those who condemn him seek the basest goals of any people on the face of the earth." Wright concludes this tirade by musing that it might

> be possible for the Negro to become reconciled to his plight
> if he could be made to believe that his sufferings were for
> some remote, high, sacrificial end; but sharing the culture
> that condemns him, and seeing that a lust for trash is what
> blinds the nation to his claims, is what sets storms to rolling
> in his soul.[31]

Yet, notwithstanding the litany of complaints Wright levels against the culture of the United States, one sentence tucked into his critique sounds a different note. As we have seen, Wright observes that Negroes lived a truer and deeper life than did the white waitresses, who existed only on "the surface of their days." Nonetheless he also expresses a wish "that Negroes, too, could live as thoughtlessly, serenely as they." That is, however superficial white life might be, it was not unthinkable to wish to trade the depth born of oppression for life's gleaming surfaces, provided that there be no more oppression—as if after all was said and done, hankering for the "trash of life" would not be the worst thing in the world provided Jim Crow were given the boot. It would be wrong to overstate the force of this wish in Wright's writings—his criticism of American society is profound and thoroughgoing. Yet, that this wish for the superficial, or for what I've also called the run-of-the-mill, finds its way into Wright's critique points again to what I've described as a feature constitutive of what we know as African American literature, namely, a fear or hope, an assertion or denial, that black difference—what Wright describes as his "culture"—was little more than a function of an oppressive society.

This being said, the goal of Wright's critique was not to assimilate African Americans into the dominant order as it was. The nature of Wright's appeal—what gives it its instrumental status—is that it presumes an audience, both black and white (albeit with the stress on the latter), that can be persuaded to recognize the integral connection between the nation's failure to realize worthwhile political, social, and moral ideals and its oppression of a minority population. Wright and the other black writers are speaking to an audience they believe possesses the capacity to recognize that merely including the Negro within American society as it exists would be tantamount to the Negro's giving up something significant—something lofty—for something tawdry, to accepting a mess of pottage for one's birthright.

In order to realize this loftier something, many black writers were expected to produce work that exhibited or presumed black difference as a distinct and needful thing, even as they acknowledged, lamented, and sought to overcome the conditions that produced that difference. Meeting this demand was a tall order. Believing that black difference would persist absent the systematic social and political constraints imposed on the nation's black population raised the specter of innate racial difference, or something close to it. During the 1920s, with the rise of what Walter Benn Michaels has termed nativist modernism, reconciling these opposing demands was facilitated by a cultural pluralism that sought to dehierarchize racial difference by ascribing unique cultures to different groups, whose respective projects were to realize the cultures of their unique groups. Groups differed because of their cultures, and the responsibility of writers was to develop their work by making it congruent with their culture. The cultural project of the moment was to realize one's identity.[32] But for satirist George Schuyler, who wrote the provocative article "Negro Art Hokum" (which served to instigate Langston Hughes's "The Negro Artist and the Racial Mountain"), as well as the novel *Black No More,* the idea that black literature could preserve black difference (or that there was a black difference to be preserved in the first place) was a scam perpetuated by a black elite for securing its dominance. *Black No More* uses the invention of a process to turn blacks into whites as an attempt to explode the belief that the experience of having lived as a despised group within American society had given black Americans a degree of moral and psychological depth and reflectiveness lacking in white society. In Schuyler's novel, rank-and-file blacks, given a chance to become white in appearance, do not hesitate to take the leap, leaving black organizations and institutions capsized in their wake. One can read *Black No More* as a book-length rejoinder to the question "What do you want?" that Du Bois poses to the audience of "Criteria." Here, however, much to Du Bois's chagrin, outracing all the cars in Cook County and throwing the richest dinners are precisely the answers his listeners would give him.

Black No More is unsentimental in its treatment of the illusion of black cultural difference and of the black elite who trade in that illusion. To be sure, after changing his skin from black to white, the central character, Max Disher, finds himself prey to some second thoughts for having left blackness behind. While visiting a cabaret for whites, he admits to finding the atmosphere "pretty dull" and recalls that blacks "enjoyed themselves more deeply and yet they were more restrained, actually more refined" than their white counterparts, whose "joy and abandon" were "obviously forced." Contrasting the "easy grace" of blacks on the dance floor to the "lumbering" white couples who were "out of step half the time and working as strenuously as stevedores emptying the bowels of a freighter," he feels "a momentary pang of mingled disgust, disillusionment and nostalgia" for black folk. This pang is "temporarily" displaced by the sight of "pretty and expensively gowned" white women, only to return a short while later when Max finds himself among a crowd of Harlem blacks, whose "jests, scraps of conversation and lusty laughter all seemed like heavenly music. Momentarily he felt a disposition to stay among them, to share again their troubles which they seemed always to bear with a lightness that was not yet indifference." This race feeling, however, does not blossom into anything like deep regret: Max "suddenly realized with just a tiny trace of remorse that the past was forever gone" and that his only recourse was "to seek his future among the Caucasians with whom he now rightfully belonged."[33] The black cultural past proves to be almost no obstacle to Max and the millions of blacks who avail themselves of the Black-No-More process.

The novel explores a further irony in portraying Dr. Junius Crookman, who invents Black-No-More, not as a victim of racial self-hatred but as "a great lover of his race":

> He had studied its history, read of its struggles and kept up
> with its achievements. He subscribed to six or seven Negro
> weekly newspapers and two of the magazines. He was so
> interested in the continued progress of the American Negroes
> that he wanted to remove all obstacles in their path by
> depriving them of their racial characteristics. His home
> and office were filled with African masks and paintings of
> Negroes by Negroes. He was what was known in Negro
> society as a Race Man. He was wedded to everything black
> except the black woman—his wife was a white girl with
> remote Negro ancestry, of the type that Negroes were wont
> to describe as being "able to pass for white." While abroad he
> had spent his spare time ransacking the libraries for facts
> about the achievements of Negroes and having liaisons with
> comely and available fraus and frauliens [sic].[34]

The satire here cuts in a number of directions, with some clear shots at Du Bois toward the end (although in the novel Du Bois is chiefly sent up in the portrait of another race leader, a Dr. Shakespeare Agamemnon Beard), and a broad swipe at the preference for lighter skin among the black elite, but the central insight is Schuyler's twinning of the idea of racial love with the disappearance of race as a social marker. In solving the "Negro Problem" for millions of black Americans, Crookman (whose name creates a degree of uneasiness about his character, which the novel never fully spells out) also turns Negro art and literature into history, so to speak.

In the novel's plot, the groups most discomfited by the transformation of race into history are the political leaders of both races. The novel sheds crocodile tears for black "Officials, [who] long since ensconced in palatial apartments, began to grow panic-stricken as pay days got farther apart," and who on "meager salaries of five thousand dollars a year . . . had fought strenuously and tirelessly to obtain for the Negroes the constitutional rights which only a few thousand rich white folk possessed. And now . . . saw the work of a lifetime being rapidly destroyed." On the other side of the disappearing color line, it is the whites who wield political and economic power in the south who are undermined by the success of Black-No-More, because to them blacks "had really been of economic, social, and psychological value," in serving "as a convenient red herring . . . when the white proletariat grew restive under exploitation," and by permitting the capitalist class and public officials to relegate segments of the population to ramshackle railway cars, streets "without sewers or pavements" and "tumble-down" apartments and houses, thereby enriching those at the top by exploiting those at the bottom. In *Black No More,* erasing the color difference between black and white changes all that. People whose demands as blacks could be conveniently ignored now find as whites that their desires and needs cannot be so easily disregarded.[35]

There is something disarmingly simple—one might even say, simplistic—in the novel's satirical solution to the race problem.

The almost childish sentiment that we'd all be better off if everyone were the same color is treated with a devilish seriousness that defies us to take it seriously. But if we are to appreciate fully the stakes of racial debate of that moment, we could do worse than take seriously the book's claim that race is only skin deep. Schuyler was writing at a time when, despite the fact that most black Americans lived lives significantly constrained by racist assumptions and practices, the intellectual and scientific tide had shifted away from biological justifications of racial difference toward an understanding of racial difference as the result of economic processes. As Jonathan Holloway writes, such major sociological scholars as Abram Harris Jr., E. Franklin Frazier, and Ralph Bunche, all of whom rose to prominence during the interwar decades, "worked steadily, if in different ways, to reorient America's obsession with the Negro problem away from an answer based upon racial solutions toward one grounded in class dynamics."[36] In 1933 all three men attended the second of two Amenia Conferences (the first was held in 1916) organized by the National Association for the Advancement of Colored People (NAACP) at Joel Spingarn's upstate New York estate where they articulated an economic view of group subordination in the United States and the world. Bunche's *A World View of Race,* published a few years later, predicted—in contradiction to Du Bois's dictum that the problem of the twentieth century was the problem of the color line—that world events for the foreseeable future would turn on class and not race relations. In *A World View,* Bunche writes, "The plain fact is that the selection of any specific physical trait or set of traits as a basis for identifying racial groups is a purely arbitrary process." To which he adds that

> though racial antagonisms constitute a serious world problem, they have no basis in biology, nor can they be accepted as the inevitable result of group difference. Such antagonisms must be analyzed and understood in their social and historical setting. Group antagonisms are social, political, and economic conflicts, not racial, though they are frequently given a racial label and seek a racial justification.

Bunche concludes, "so class will some day supplant race in world affairs. Race war then will be merely a side-show to the gigantic class war which will be waged in the big tent we call the world."[37] The 1930s was also, of course, the decade when, influenced by the Communist Left, Langston Hughes made his political and aesthetic turn to poetry that cast the problems besetting black Americans in terms that highlighted their status as oppressed workers. Accordingly, Schuyler's imaginary dissolving of racial difference to bring into view a world structured along lines of economic domination should nonetheless be understood as standing within, rather than outside of, black intellectual thought of the moment.

That is, Schuyler's turning blacks into whites for the purpose of illuminating the nation's social landscape is consistent with the narrative devices employed by a host of black authors who, by creating characters of mixed lineages, perform genealogically what Schuyler does through biotechnology, namely give black people the right to choose to be black or white. Schuyler differs from most of his predecessors (as well as his successors I might add), however, in that he not only presumes that blacks would choose to be white if they could but also in that he does not condemn them for doing so or convict them of self-hatred for making the choice. In fact, what rules out self-hatred as a problem is that in the logic of Schuyler's novel, blacks who become black-no-more are not denying themselves but merely revealing themselves as what they already were, namely "lamp-blacked Anglo Saxons."

In fact, self-denial in the novel turns out to be all on the "white" side of the ledger, as we discover when a genealogical scheme perpetrated by two of the novel's white supremacists, who are leaders of the Anglo-Saxon Association of America, backfires. Unable to tell by skin color the differences between white and black, they assume that genealogy will tell. Poised to reassert race through genealogical statistics, Mr. Samuel Buggerie discovers instead that

> These statistics we've gathered prove that most of our social
> leaders, especially of Anglo-Saxon lineage, are descendants
> of colonial stock that came here in bondage. They associated
> with slaves, in many cases worked and slept with them. They
> intermixed with the blacks and the women were socially
> exploited by their masters. Then, even more than today, the
> illegitimate birth rate was very high in America.[38]

This discovery is made just in the nick of time to save Max from having to tell Helen, his racist, pregnant wife, that he is not really white. Instead the data reveal that Helen, whose refusal to date "niggers" was one of the reasons behind Max's decision to undergo the Black-No-More process, is herself black. Ironically, this turn in the novel's plot required little inventiveness on Schuyler's part: Walter A. Plecker, the first registrar of Virginia's Bureau of Vital Statistics and the driving force behind that state's 1924 "Racial Integrity Act," which made it "unlawful for any white person in this State to marry any save a white person, or a person with no other admixture of blood than white and American Indian," undertook a study similar to that described in Schuyler's novel with equally embarrassing results.[39] Schuyler titled his novel *Black No More,* but *White No More* would have done as well, as indicated by both Buggerie's statistical findings and the novel's concluding scene, in which everyone is trying to make themselves just a little browner in the wake of another discovery by Crookman that "in practically every instance the new Caucasians were from two to three shades lighter than the old Caucasians."[40]

The ambiguity of the novel's ending, in which race consciousness appears to be just as strong as ever among the nation's populace, coupled with various grudging or indifferent responses by the novel's critics over the years, has led some of *Black No More*'s most astute recent readers to reach conclusions that bear helpfully on the argument here. On the one hand, what I've described as Schuyler's indifference to the idea of black culture has prompted Gene Jarrett to assert that as the skin color of the novel's characters "becomes black no more, through fantasy and satire, *Black No More*'s textual color also becomes black no more, to the extent that the novel, in a sense, becomes black literature no more."[41] By contrast, Jeffrey B. Ferguson insists that resistance to orthodoxy has been constitutive of Schuyler's career in a way that makes him and his work "representative."[42] Accordingly, for Ferguson, despite the novel's freewheeling satire:

> Black No More celebrates the integrity of black American communal life under segregation, which [it] derides blacks themselves for underrating in their rush to join the greedy and indistinguishable members of the vast American herd. In Black No More taking Crookman's formula is the act of a fool.

The novel, in Ferguson's estimation, champions "the hard-won values that make [black] group life worthy of dissemination" and the "qualities that made blacks resilient, one might even say triumphant, under difficult environmental circumstances."[43]

In declaring Black No More an outlier, Jarrett intimates that Schuyler's novel did not receive the critical acclaim it should have enjoyed. But as Ferguson's survey of the immediate critical reception of the novel reveals, despite the divergent assessments that often attend a bitingly satirical work, there were enough positive reviews of the novel to warrant calling it a successful work of African American fiction in its moment.[44] Nor did the novel entirely disappear from critical consideration in the ensuing decades. Indeed, in 1950 a critic writing in *Phylon* deemed Black No More a "minor classic." Nevertheless, despite Jarrett's overstatement, he is onto something in noting that the novel raises important questions about how African American literature ought to be defined and in insisting that an accurate description of African American literature ought to include *Black No More* and other "white life" fiction without rendering them anomalous. While, for his part, Ferguson is right in declaring Schuyler and his work "representative," they are not representative quite in the ways he suggests. That is, although *Black No More* destroys any illusions that white society is somehow better than black society, which as we have seen above is a standard critique within African American literature, it doesn't produce much in the way of grounds for preferring black society. Beyond the ease and grace exhibited by black dancers on the dance floor and "the music, laughter, gaiety, jesting and abandon" of the "Negro ghetto"—that is, beyond the realm of expressive and leisure culture—the novel depicts or alludes to little that represents the "integrity of black life," save Madeline Scranton, the wife of Bunny Brown, Max Fisher's best friend, who is mentioned briefly only near the end of the novel as "the last black gal in the country" and a "race patriot." Madeline, however, plays virtually no role in the novel's plot.[45] In fact, those characters who speak directly of the "integrity of Negro society" and the race's "marvelous record of achievement since emancipation" are the black leaders whose well-being depended on being able to count on the support of the black rank and file.[46] And when the narrator laments that Black-No-More has caused ordinary black people to forget "all loyalties, affiliations, and responsibilities," he quickly undermines that lament by listing organizations and individuals whose viability had been a by-product of black subordination, the "Negro politicians in the various Black Belts, grown fat and sleek 'protecting' vice with the aid of Negro votes which they were able to control by virtue of housing segregation."

Of course, if one reads the novel's conclusion as demonstrating the durability of the nation's ongoing commitment to racial domination of some sort or another, then it might be right to infer that the key lesson to be drawn from *Black No More* is the folly of abandoning the values that had proved "resilient" under "difficult environmental circumstances." Indeed a prominent strain of recent black culturalist scholarship associated with such scholars as Paul Gilroy and Robin D. G. Kelley would insist that we ought to view the loss of black cultural spaces described in the novel as profound, because it was in such spaces that black solidarity and opposition to Jim Crow and oppression developed and were nurtured. In Kelley's words, the congregating that occurred in places of leisure and worship enabled "black communities to construct and enact a sense of solidarity; to fight with each other; to maintain and struggle over a collective memory of oppression and pleasure, degradation and dignity; to debate what it means to be 'black,' 'Negro,' 'colored,' and so forth."[47] For Gilroy, the most transformative features of black politics are transacted in the idiom of black music, which he credits with having produced a "distinctive counterculture of modernity."[48] While there is no gainsaying, generally, the possibility that leisure spaces and activities may permit exploration of behaviors and ideas proscribed in other social arenas, the pertinence of this social fact is limited in any consideration of *Black No More*. In the novel, the black Americans who most frequently avail themselves of these activities and leisure places prove no more resistant to the blandishments of Black-No-More than do those blacks who would have found such places anathema. The claim that such spaces promote black solidarity could make sense only as a lament that the black working class is abandoning the very things that made them a people—the kind of lament that finds voice in Jean Toomer's "regret" in the 1920s that black "folk-spirit was walking in to die on the modern desert" or Cornel West's warning in the 1990s that "the cultural structures that once sustained black life in America are no longer able to fend off the nihilistic threat" he sees as plaguing black life in the late twentieth century. Yet there is little space for such worry in *Black No More,* where whitened blacks become just as neurotic as other whites—no better, no worse.

Part of what makes it unnecessary in the novel to consider the consequences of prematurely abandoning the culture that in the past presumably provided respite from racism is that in *Black No More,* race is quickly becoming a thing of the past. To be sure, skin color continues to matter in the world of the novel, and Crookman's announcement that paler skin is now the new black precipitates a set of responses that briefly recapitulate the history of racism and racial protest, including caricatures, letters to newspaper editors, appeals to the president, and the like—all of which gets narrated in a couple of pages under the heading "AND SO ON AND SO ON," an apparent indication that the more things change, the more they stay the same. Yet in making skin color the only thing that matters, Crookman's invention short-circuits the device that allows race, particularly in fiction, to work in the first place. To understand why this is so, one need only consider the many apparently white characters who populate African American literature. For these characters, the problem is not that they don't look white. Rather the problem is that looking white does not seem to be enough to make them white (or to put it another way, that being black doesn't require that one look black). These novels present race as being more than skin deep even as they attempt to strike a blow against Jim Crow by insisting that any difference between black and white people is merely superficial.

Black No More stresses the superficiality of racial difference common to black fiction while treating the argument that race is deeper than skin color as little more than class ideology serving the interests of black elites and their white southern counterparts. The novel poses the question characteristic of (if often implicit in) African American literature, namely, what would become of black life absent the discriminatory practices required of Jim Crow? The difference that makes *Black No More* appear to be an outlier to the project of African American literature is the tone of its answer, which treats with irreverence what other novels regard as tragedy. Indeed, the concluding portion of Schuyler's novel reroutes any tragic impulse with a brutal piece of poetic justice in which the white Democratic leadership and heads of the Anglo-Saxon Association of America, Arthur Snobbcraft and Dr. Samuel Buggerie, are lynched when their scheme to tar the Republican Party leadership with the stain of black ancestry backfires. Because the press circulates pictures of both men nationwide, Snobbcraft and Buggerie find themselves in the unenviable position of being almost the only apparently white men in the country who can be identified as black. Attempting to escape by plane to Mexico where Snobbcraft owns a ranch, both men end up instead in the backwoods of Mississippi, where the plane is forced to land after running out of gas. Aware that they are now at ground zero of American racial hatred, they decide to disguise themselves by "blacking up," because, by Snobbcraft's reasoning, "real niggers are scarce now and nobody would think of bothering a couple of them, even in Mississippi." Snobbcraft, however, is unaware that a local preacher in the town of Happy Hill, afraid of losing his flock to other congregations, has been praying to God for "a nigger for his congregation to lynch" as "marked evidence of his power."[49] When Snobbcraft and Buggerie are seized by the crowd, they do manage to forestall their fate temporarily by demonstrating that their faces are merely blackened. But when someone who has seen the newspapers informs the crowd that the two men in their custody are indeed the Democratic leaders who have been identified as black, the lynching begins again with gusto.

In the vision of *Black No More,* the world in which race is more than skin deep—in which even if whiteness is valued, it is not enough to show a white skin in order to save one's skin—is a world in which no sane person would want to live. Of course, what makes the novel a difficult pill to swallow is that it also demonstrates that in a world where what matters is merely skin color, an attribute that (in this novel) can be changed to suit the prevailing prejudices and fashion, the scramble for preferment and advantage continues unabated—that even when race no longer matters, all sorts of inequalities can still count in American social life.

Like all other African American literature, *Black No More* was written within a context in which all involved were unavoidably trying to figure out just what sort of problem Jim Crow presented to those engaged in creative work. There was indeed no consensus on how literature ought to respond to the social and legal reality of segregation, even down to whether or not black writers should see Jim Crow as the biggest social problem facing black Americans. Nonetheless, black literature was an imaginative response not merely to the lived reality but also to the legal fact of segregation. Consequently, black writers anticipated that a change in that legal reality would dramatically affect not only their social reality but also the literature that had been produced in response to it. Whatever the virtues they found in black life as it had been lived since emancipation, and whatever the shortcomings that characterized the dominant white society around them—including the literature produced by that society—black writers knew that their work had been produced within constraints and that, as those constraints weakened, their writing would be expected to change.

Another way of putting this is to say that despite the attention given to the folk past and the artistic achievements of past greats whose work had gone unacknowledged, African American literature was prospective rather than retrospective. The past was indeed important, but primarily as a way of refuting charges of black inferiority and only secondarily as a source and guide for ongoing creative activity. In the main, writers and critics tended to speak as if the best work had not been written but was yet to come, and the shape of that work was yet to be determined. Indeed, if anything separates what African American literature is now from what it was, that difference, ironically, can be summed up by quoting that most American of American writers, Ralph Waldo Emerson: "Our age is retrospective."

2

PARTICULARITY AND THE PROBLEM OF INTERPRETATION

All around us today the air resounds with calls to integrate the Negro into our national life. Very probably the increasingly favorable reaction to those calls is a sign that both America and its Negroes are reaching a certain maturity. Negro writers are promising to do their bit in keeping pace with the latest trend. Symptomatically, they are losing as never quite before, their exaggerated self-consciousness. . . . The Negro writer, who has always been very American, even in his failings and despite his handicaps, is still responsive to his environment.[1]

Blyden Jackson's easy acceptance of what might be termed an integrationist imperative was characteristic of many of the essays on literature that appeared in the fourth number of the eleventh volume of *Phylon* in 1950, a special issue titled "The Negro in Literature: The Current Scene." Founded by W. E. B. Du Bois and published by Clark Atlanta University, *Phylon* was a major venue for the publication of literary, cultural, and historical scholarship on race. Its contributors were frequently among the most prominent scholars, both black and white, writing about the idea of race relations in the United States and around the world. Guiding the journal's editorial practices was a belief that scholarship and literature could help move society further along the road to racial equality and that trends in literature often reflected broader social changes. Accordingly, for this special issue, editors Mozell C. Hill and M. Carl Holman asked an illustrious group of black writers and critics to respond to such questions as:

> What are the promising and unpromising aspects of the Negro's present position in American literature? Are there any aspects of the life of the Negro in America which seem deserving of franker, or deeper, or more objective treatment? Does current literature by and about Negroes seem more or less propagandistic than before? Would you agree with those who feel that the Negro writer, the Negro as subject, and the Negro critic and scholar are moving toward an "unlabeled" future in which they will be measured without regard to racial origin and conditioning?[2]

The various responses to these questions were parceled out in the issue's several sections under such headings as "The Negro Writer Looks at His World," "Fiction and Folklore," "Poetry," and "The Van Vechten Revolution" (in which George Schuyler praised white novelist and critic Carl Van Vechten for leading the way in encouraging white elites to accept their black counterparts as equals). Jackson's essay appeared in a section titled "Criticism and Literary Scholarship." Articles by several other writers, including Hugh M. Gloster, J. Saunders Redding, Nick Aaron Ford, Charles H. Nichols Jr., L. D. Reddick, G. Lewis Chandler, N. P. Tillman, and Ira De A. Reid, were grouped under the title "Symposium: Survey and Forecast." Alain Locke provided a summary statement.

Jackson's receptive response to Hill and Holman's suggestion that an "unlabeled" future for black American literature might be possible resonated among a broad section of writers and intellectuals of the moment. To be sure, not all of the issue's contributors fully embraced this vision of the future. For example, Arna Bontemps, whose essay appeared in the "Poetry" section, constrasted Harlem Renaissance poets to their 1950 successors by remarking:

> But in those days a good many of the group went to The Dark Tower to weep because they felt an injustice in the critics' insistence upon calling them Negro poets instead of just poets. That attitude was particularly displeasing to Countee Cullen. But some who are writing today are not so sure. Considering the general state of poetry, the isolation of so many major poets from the everyday problems of mankind, their private language, their rarified metaphysical subject matter, one or two Negroes have even dared to suggest that being a Negro poet may not be so bad after all.[3]

But if black particularity had not disappeared from the projected future of black writing, as discussed in the *Phylon* special issue, the willingness of its various contributors to contemplate without horror the future of an American literature without a special category for black literature is certainly worth noting in relation to both the past and the future of *Phylon*.

A decade beyond its founding, *Phylon* was not, in 1950, mining quite the same cultural and political vein it had prospected when W. E. B. Du Bois had led the way in bringing it into existence in 1940. That year had also seen the publication of Du Bois's autobiographical volume, *Dusk of Dawn,* which Du Bois provocatively subtitled *An Essay toward an Autobiography of a Race Concept.* It was hardly coincidental. In fact, appreciating how dramatically the orientation of *Phylon* in 1950 differed from its guiding vision at its founding requires some familiarity with Du Bois's thinking from the mid-1930s, when he breaks officially with the National Association for the Advancement of Colored People (NAACP), until 1940, when both *Phylon* and *Dusk of Dawn* make their appearances. In the latter text, Du Bois reiterates the reasons behind his break with the NAACP, explaining:

> When the NAACP was formed, the great mass of Negro children were being trained in Negro schools; the great mass of Negro churchgoers were members of Negro churches; the great mass of Negro citizens lived in Negro neighborhoods; the great mass of Negro voters voted with the same political party; and the mass of Negroes joined with Negroes and co-operated with Negroes in order to fight the extension of this segregation and to move toward better conditions. What was true in 1910 was still true in 1940 and will be true in 1970. But with this vast difference: that the segregated Negro

institutions are better organized, more intelligently planned and more efficiently conducted, and today form in themselves the best and most compelling argument for the ultimate abolition of the color line.[4]

It is virtually impossible upon reading this passage not to be impressed by the many ways in which Du Bois seems prescient about the present moment. Although black children are no longer educated in legally segregated schools, a significant number still attend schools that are predominantly black.[5] The nation's church congregations remain noticeably segregated (although the advent of megachurches may be making inroads into church demographics). Even President Barack Obama, before the controversial remarks of his former pastor, the Reverend Jeremiah Wright, forced him to seek another place of worship, attended a church where most of his fellow congregants were African American. And it is still the case that an overwhelming majority of black voters cast their votes for candidates of one party.

Yet however accurate Du Bois's predictions about the late twentieth and early twenty-first centuries may seem, it is just as important to register how his prognostications are not entirely right. In fact, there is a decisive way in which Du Bois's moment differs from our own: although many black Americans still live in predominantly black neighborhoods and many black schoolchildren still attend predominantly black schools, for rather clear reasons it is the case that African American social life and participation in social and political institutions are no longer oriented around a fight against segregation. For now, we should acknowledge that in Du Bois's eyes it was the persistence of segregation, and white America's commitment to it, that demanded a reassessment of the problem of the color line he had articulated at the beginning of the twentieth century. Over the first three decades of the twentieth century, Du Bois had believed that the commitment to racial segregation and the justifications supporting it could be successfully countered by evidence across the range of human endeavor that a belief in black inferiority was irrational. But by the time he came to write *Dusk of Dawn,* he was persuaded by the growing prominence of Freudianism in Western intellectual circles, the irrational horror of national socialism in Germany, and the popularity of social science works such as William Graham Summer's *Folkways and Mores* (well known for such conservative nostrums as "Stateways can't change folkways")[6] that, as far as race was concerned, the ultimate realization of the Enlightenment project of displacing ignorance with knowledge, and superstition with rational thought, lay further in the future than he had assumed. The new problem to be faced, as he wrote in *Dusk of Dawn,* was that most human actions "are not rational and many of them arise from subconscious urges." The key consequence of Du Bois's "discovery" that the irrational played a greater role in the race problem than previously imagined was that a change in tactics was unavoidable. He reasons,

> The present attitude and action of the whole world is not
> based solely upon rational, deliberate intent. It is a matter of
> conditioned reflexes; of long followed habits, customs and

folkways; of subconscious trains of reasoning and unconscious nervous reflexes. To attack and better all this calls for
more than appeal and argument. It needs carefully planned
and scientific propaganda.[7]

As we have seen, propaganda is not a word that Du Bois shies
away from. Declaring, "All Art is propaganda and ever must be,"
he told an NAACP audience in 1926, "I stand in utter shameless-
ness and say that whatever art I have for writing has been used
always for propaganda for gaining the right of black folk to
love and enjoy. I do not care a damn for any art that is not used
for propaganda."[8] As he also noted in 1935 in *Black Reconstruction,* the same held for history, which he describes as "a field
devastated by passion and belief."[9] But regardless of the field of
endeavor, the need for black propaganda was dictated by a social order in which, as Du Bois saw it, all the propaganda had
been one-sided in favor of whites. His intent was to impress on
black writers and scholars that it was long past time to right
the imbalance.

Through the 1920s Du Bois had reason to believe that a transformation of the world's racial order lay just beyond the horizon. In his 1929 novel *Dark Princess,* which he claimed to be his
favorite book, he allows his title character to predict, "In 1952,
the Dark World goes free."[10] By the 1940s, however, he saw the
liberation of the darker world as having receded into the distant future. Accordingly, the prospect that black Americans
for the foreseeable future would likely operate in a segregated
world called for a shift in emphasis in his cultural politics.

Responding to a vision of a world based more on unreason than reason, he placed even more stress on Negro art as a tool "not to amuse the white audience, but to inspire and direct the acting Negro group itself."[11] Although a hortatory dimension of black culture had been a feature of Du Bois's thought from the outset—particularly in such essays as "The Conservation of Races," in which he argued that it was "the duty of the Americans of Negro descent, as a body to maintain their race identity until [the] mission of the Negro people is accomplished, and the ideal of human brotherhood has become a practical possibility"—cooperation across the color line among the elites of both groups received equal emphasis in his turn-of-the-century writing.[12] In *The Souls of Black Folk* he insists, "Only by a union of intelligence and sympathy across the color-line in this critical period of the Republic shall justice and right triumph."[13] By contrast, as constitutionally sanctioned segregation neared its half-century anniversary, the role of black elites in developing semiautonomous black organizations struck him as the best long-term strategy in combating segregation. Thus it is helpful to see *Dusk of Dawn* and *Phylon* as cultural, scholarly, and autobiographical propaganda in favor of Du Bois's commitment at that time to establishing Negro consumer cooperatives as a way of creating an "industrial and cultural democracy," a point he emphasizes in the concluding chapter of *Dusk of Dawn* when he recalls that after completing the writing of *Black Reconstruction* in 1935, "I naturally turned my thoughts toward putting into permanent form that economic program of the Negro which I believed should succeed." That program is laid out in what he titles the Basic American Negro Creed, which lauds "unity of racial effort," and predicts, "If carefully and intelligently planned, a cooperative Negro industrial system in America can be established in the midst of and in conjunction with the surrounding national industrial organization."[14]

Du Bois's activities around and subsequent to the publication of *Dusk of Dawn* were continuous with his plan to establish this "black, cooperative rural economy in the South, led by the Talented Tenth."[15] In addition to founding *Phylon,* he met in Chicago with the presidents of black land-grant colleges to propose an interinstitutional social science study of southern blacks, was selected to coordinate the project, and subsequently organized a conference in Atlanta. In consolidating his efforts around the consumer cooperative project, he had reserved a major role for the study of black art and literature. His challenge to the NAACP Board of Directors to endorse his proposal that the Negro as "a group must make up its mind to associate and co-operate for its own uplift and in defense of its self respect," concluded by asking the Board:

> Does it believe in Negro business enterprise of any sort?
> Does it believe in Negro history, Negro literature and
> Negro art?
> Does it believe in the Negro spirituals?[16]

Although not quite syllogistic in form, Du Bois's series of questions implies that the need and justification for some degree of economic self-determination logically follows from an acknowledgment that blacks had developed distinctive forms of cultural expression. Even so, Du Bois took care to point out that this turn toward racial group self-determination was itself determined more by external pressure than by some internal law of group self-development. He writes, "This is and is designed to be a program of racial effect and this narrowed goal is forced on us today by the unyielding determination of the mass of the white race to enslave, exploit and insult Negroes."[17] Thus, for Du Bois at this moment, the intransigence of those forces benefiting from the maintenance of Jim Crow meant that for the foreseeable future, black studies would be carried out largely in Negro colleges oriented toward the goal of creating a Negro cooperative economy, and black literature would be nourished from the same institutional base. If Du Bois seemed prescient in predicting how durable de facto segregation would be in the ensuing decades, his expectation that African American studies would continue to be nurtured primarily within Negro colleges was largely not on target. As Noliwe Rooks has recently demonstrated, the current prominence of African American studies derives from an awareness of the usefulness of the discipline to campus race-relations management. Rooks observes, "African American Studies (then termed Black Studies) was envisioned and proposed by the Ford Foundation as a means [in the 1970s] to desegregate and integrate the student bodies, faculties, and curricula of colleges and universities in ways that would mirror the public school systems that had been ordered by the Supreme Court to free themselves from 'separate but equal' racial education systems."[18]

That the major centers of black studies today are in places like Harvard, Princeton, and Yale rather than, say, the Atlanta University Center, marks a significant difference between Du Bois's moment and the present.

The cast of Du Bois's thinking in 1940 is evident in the first issue of *Phylon,* which begins, as did *Dusk of Dawn,* with an "Apology" explaining its employment of the terms "race" and "culture." According to the editors, the journal will use

> both designations more or less interchangeably; because it would emphasize that view of race which regards it as cultural and historical in essence, rather than primarily biological and psychological. Because of the reality back of it, we continue the use of the older concept of the word "race," referring to the greater groups of human kind which by outer pressure and inner cohesiveness, still form and have long formed a stronger or weaker unity of thought and action. Among these groups appear both biological and psychological likenesses, although we believe that these aspects have in the past been overemphasized in the face of many contradictory facts. While, therefore, we continue to study and measure all human differences we seem to see the basis of real and practical racial unity in culture. We use then the old word in new containers. A culture consists of the ideas, habits and values, the technical processes and goods which any group becomes possessed of either by inheritance or adoption.

> Looking over the world today we see as incentive to economic gain, as cause of war, and as infinite source of

cultural inspiration nothing so important as race and group contact. Here if anywhere the leadership of science is demanded not to obliterate all race and group distinctions, but to know and study them, to see and appreciate them at their true values, to emphasize the use and place of human differences as tool and method of progress; to make straight the path to a common world humanity through the development of cultural gifts to their highest possibilities.[19]

Reflecting the new consensus that biological, and in this case psychological, explanations of race had been discredited, the "Apology" nonetheless insists on the ongoing utility of culture and race, terms that the editors employ interchangeably, in achieving social and political progress. If there is a hint of the "unlabeled" future, it resides only in the notion of "common world humanity" adduced by the editors as an eventual future and eventual goal. The immediate and midterm intellectual project remains the same as it had been when Du Bois wrote "The Conservation of Races," namely, to "appreciate" race distinctions in order to develop cultural gifts that could then be contributed to the project of realizing common world humanity. Broader values would have to be pursued through, and not against, race.

By contrast, although race remained very much on the minds of the writers who contributed to *Phylon* a decade later, and who still tended in some way to link black American writers' individual achievement in the novel to the notion of group progress (an indication of the indexical feature constitutive of the black literary project), the standard by which they charted progress tended not to be the development of a unique group sensibility. Instead they noted the individual freedom enjoyed by a new generation of writers who were progressively more able to take advantage of the increasing social freedoms that postwar civil rights gains were making possible. Remarking that as an "expression 'Negro literature' finds less acceptance among intellectual circles than ever before and that the Negro novelist, writing for both whites and Negroes, is realizing more and more that these two audiences are in actuality one," Thomas D. Jarrett, in an article titled "Unfettered Creativity: A Note on the Negro Novelist's Coming of Age," observes:

> More and more, it seems to me, no matter what the subject is, it cannot be gainsaid that before Negro fiction attains full maturity there must be a growing social consciousness and a universality in the treatment of themes; and, concomitantly, there must be a higher regard for literary values if works that are meaningful and vital and of the first order are to be produced.[20]

The extent to which writers were able to dispense with the realization of black group sensibility as a mission can be gauged in part by the fact that they sometimes included writing by whites in the category of what they termed race literature. "The Literature of the Negro," to quote the subtitle of an article by Alain Locke in the first number of *Phylon*'s 1950 volume, was just as likely to include fiction by white writers who wrote with sensitivity about race, even on an international scale. Locke and others were positively impressed by Alan Paton's *Cry, the Beloved Country* as well as by William Faulkner's *Intruder in the Dust*, the former of which Locke describes as "sheet-lightning revelation."[21] Moving across the boundaries of literary and popular fiction, film, poetry, and drama, Locke orients his discussion not in terms of the expression of a group consciousness but in terms of an apparently dissolving boundary between writers of different races, enabling black and white authors alike to treat a broad range of topics with what he saw as subtlety and honesty.

As many scholars have argued, Locke's outlook reflected the broader mood of the time. Richard H. King observes,

> In the wake of World War II, a universalist vision in which the different races were understood to be equal in natural capacities and legal-political rights became a consensus position among intellectual and scientific elites in the West. . . . Much of postwar American life was marked by a quest for a general consensus on values and behavior and a commitment to a national version of universality.[22]

The sentiments expressed in the eleventh volume of *Phylon*, while remaining open to the usefulness of racial particularity, fell in line with the consensus facilitated by Gunnar Myrdal's *An American Dilemma*. Early in the 1940s, recognizing that the race problem was a growing embarrassment to a nation that was fashioning itself as the moral and political leader of the free world, the Carnegie Corporation commissioned Swedish social scientist Gunnar Myrdal to conduct a comprehensive study of the black/white problem in American society, which resulted in the publication of Myrdal's massive study in 1944. Myrdal put forward a view that the Negro problem represented an anomaly in American political and social life because most white Americans believed in an American creed loosely derived from the nation's founding documents. They held to the rightness of that creed and recognized at some level that their treatment of the Negro stood in contradiction to, and could not be rationalized under it. Myrdal also insisted that blacks were not a foreign entity but had derived a set of semiautonomous institutions in reaction to the racial exclusion of American society and therefore could be easily assimilated to that society once the barriers of exclusion had fallen.[23]

It takes little imagination to see how a consensus crystallizing around Myrdal's analysis took the wind out of the sails of the cooperative venture outlined in *Dusk of Dawn*. Not only, as David Levering Lewis suggests, did the funding of Myrdal's study mean that another of Du Bois's projects, his *Encyclopedia of the Negro,* went unsupported, it also drew into its orbit many of the major black social scientists just at the moment Du Bois was trying to pull together his land grant college–based social study of the Negro.[24] Additionally, Myrdal's study suggested that white opinion was more tractable and less deeply irrational on matters of race than Du Bois was asserting, and it also insisted that administering the "Negro problem" could remain a matter of interracial cooperation at a time when Du Bois was arguing that it should, for the time being, be an intraracial matter.

Yet, however ascendant the new consensus seemed by 1950, the relative obscurity of *Phylon*'s "The Negro in Literature" tells a slightly different story. This issue of the journal did not enjoy the future that its editors had imagined for it. Hill and Holman closed their Preface by expressing hope that "this issue of PHYLON 'will be a major contribution to critical writing on the Negro.'"[25] Testifying to their ambition was their having asked Alain Locke to provide the summary statement for their symposium. Twenty-five years earlier Locke had edited the special issue of *Survey Graphic* that had become *The New Negro*, the volume credited with ushering in the Harlem Renaissance. Hill and Holman's decision to ask for Locke's summary underscored their historical ambitions for their symposium, and Locke shared their belief in the significance of the collection, describing it as an advance on the agenda of *The New Negro*. In Locke's estimation, "these eight essays analyzing our literary output and its implications mark a considerable step forward toward objective self-criticism. This is a necessary and welcome sign of cultural maturity. It was predicated twenty-five years ago as one of the objectives of the so-called Negro Renaissance." In celebrating this symposium as a milestone, Locke did not feel that racial particularity was simply to be abandoned. Instead he felt black life offered much that was artistically promising, arguing that as long as "racial themes" were taken up "by choice" and not imposed on black writers, "it still remains that Negro life and experience contain one of the unworked mines of American dramatic and fictional material." The matter to be determined was not whether African American writers should write about African Americans, but rather under what conditions and in which way ought they to do so. And for this, Locke had a ready slogan. "Give us Negro life and experience in all the arts but with a third dimension of universalized common-denominator humanity."[26] Indeed, five years later, shortly after Locke's death, Charles S. Johnson, who along with Locke had helped create the Harlem Renaissance, concluded a conference assessing Locke's *The New Negro* thirty years after its publication, with the following assertion:

> We have in this present period, and out of the matrix of the Renaissance period, scholars who know the cultural process, and savants who have imbibed the best that civilization can offer and can and are aiding human knowledge, within the context, not of a special culture group, but of the national society and world civilization.[27]

The "third dimension of common-denominator humanity" embraced by so many of the essays in the *Phylon* symposium seemed on its way to becoming Locke's epitaph.

Yet despite the hopes expressed by editor and contributor alike that the fourth number of *Phylon*'s 1950 issue would be reckoned a high-water mark for African American literary and critical practice, it is worth noting that up to the current moment, neither it nor any of the essays published in it have achieved anything approaching the visibility of *The New Negro,* which, by contrast, has become a fixture in the study of African American literature. In fact, it is arguable that since *The New Negro,* only three or four edited collections—Larry Neal and

Amiri Baraka's *Black Fire* in 1968, Addison Gayle's *The Black Aesthetic* in 1972, and Henry Louis Gates Jr.'s *"Race," Writing, and Difference,* which began as two special issues of *Critical Inquiry*—have had a field-defining effect with respect to the discussion of African American literature comparable to Locke's earlier volume. And despite Gates's commitment to not making the racial identity of the author a factor in determining the contributors to his volume (a fact that also characterized Locke's approach to *The New Negro*), what his volume shares with those of the 1960s is a commitment not to an "unlabeled" future but to a future in which the specificity or particularity of black literature would constitute the critical focal point for discussions of black expressive culture.

The resurgence of racial particularity in the 1970s, following the emphasis on universalism in the 1950s, has produced a variety of narratives. Richard H. King, for example, argues that "by the 1960s in the United States, universalism was increasingly challenged by cultural particularism," and that those making this argument insisted that "Myrdal's American Creed no longer fit the social or cultural reality of America, if it ever had." As a consequence,

> African American intellectuals and political activists increasingly agreed with the point that W. E. B. Du Bois, who died in 1963, had spent his whole life making: the group was more important than the individual, and race was a necessary destiny rather than a contingent burden. By the end of the decade, the overlapping emergence of a black consciousness,

black arts, and black power movements testified to a new level of political and cultural self-awareness among America's black population. After 1965, "Negroes" became "blacks" and black became "beautiful."[28]

As had been the case when Locke wrote the introduction to *The New Negro* in the mid-1920s, the sense among intellectuals and writers that profound transformations were taking place in the day-to-day lives and the sensibilities of large segments of the black population raised the question of how well literary and critical practice reflected or prescribed popular opinion or belief. Locke and his fellow Renaissance writers had been emboldened by the first great migration of southern blacks to northern cities, an apparent mass movement in which in "a real sense it is the rank and file who are leading, and the leaders who are following."[29] They viewed this transformation as indicating that old representations of black sensibility no longer served and that their own position in the urban centers of the north uniquely positioned them to produce an art more broadly representative of mass desires. The tenuousness of this claim, however, was evident in the volume that was making it. There was no firm agreement among the authors on just which aesthetic forms best distilled the mass spirit. Countee Cullen's poem "Heritage" sought to link black distinctiveness to "the song / Sung by wild barbaric birds" in an Africa "three centuries removed" from the present, while Locke himself described the aesthetic of Africa as "rigid, controlled, disciplined, abstract, heavily conventionalized" and contrasted it with the "emotional temper of the American Negro."[30] Jean Toomer in his poem "The Song of the Sun" found the heart of black sensibility in "A song-lit race of slaves" on whom the sun was setting.[31] Meanwhile the white anthropologist Melville Herskovits, stating an opinion he was later to reverse, declared black cultural life to be of "the same pattern, only a different shade" as white life.[32] Indeed Locke's introductory essay made it clear that for all its celebration of the black rank and file, *The New Negro* laid out a plan of race-relations management directed by black elites. Warning his readers of the possibility of continued social upheavals where the races came into contact with one another, Locke declared, "The only safeguard for mass relations in the future must be provided in the carefully maintained contact of the enlightened minorities of both race groups."[33]

Like its predecessor, the movement among black writers in the late 1960s and early 1970s to define black particularity insisted on its hostility to the outmoded representational regimes of previous elites and its commitment to art identified with the black working classes. Yet while there is still lively debate among scholars about how successful Black Power and Black Aesthetic writers and spokespersons were in shaping an oppositional practice, the writers from these movements did not essentially break from the "elite-brokerage politics" that defined the Harlem Renaissance era. Whatever else such a politics may entail, necessary to its operation are competing claims about the collective nature of the black population and withering assessments of the aspirations of one group or another to represent this collectivity. The cultural politics associated with these debates (and these are debates in which culture is necessarily paramount) confront the interpretive challenge of relating black literary texts to the desires, dispositions, and situation of the larger population. Accordingly, critics have not been at all shy about evaluating literary works by declaring them in or out of tune with the black population as a whole—evaluations that, by and large, have not been accompanied by much in the way of evidence for the conclusions they draw. Instead, broad characterizations of the black population as, for example, group-oriented rather than individualistic have tended to be proffered as reasons for preferring one writer to another.

Institutional literary criticism has always stood in a problematic relationship to the works on which it focuses and the public to which it interprets those works. Critics generally designate as part of a nation's literature those works that are presumed to reflect or express a people's identity. Yet at the same time, by advocating for the teaching of canonical literature, scholars tacitly acknowledge the marginality of this corpus to the reading habits of the general populace. In other words, the myth of a national literature claims that it merely expresses what a nation already is, but that until and unless the people learn the literature that somehow already expresses them, they will not know who they are. Leslie Fiedler's 1982 polemic *What Was Literature? Culture and Mass Society,* to which the title of this book alludes, argues that literary criticism has unfortunately severed its ties to a broader reading public by committing itself to keeping alive those works it deemed to have aesthetic merit over those that enjoy popularity with a broader reading public.[34] For the moment I mean the allusion here to be only a faint one, because the analysis I am pursuing does not hinge on favoring popular over elite tastes. Rather, the usefulness of considering Fiedler in relation to African American literature is that doing so helps make clear that whether or not black scholars charged the literary establishment with overlooking African American works in general, or with favoring only those works that conformed to dominant standards, the posture available to insurgent black critics was that of championing the popular against the highbrow, black against white, or working-class black people against compromised black elites. Unlike Fiedler, however, black critics did not have to contend that the term "popular literature" referred to works that were widely read by blacks (in part because they could argue that popular black literary taste had been corrupted by sellout black elites), but instead they merely had to claim that certain works, by virtue of evincing certain properties, many of which were common to forms of music that actually were popular, expressed the identity of black people. My point is not that none of the works championed by vernacular critics were or are popular. Rather I want to underscore that the work accomplished by these critiques has been to turn "elite" and "popular" into formal categories—instead of assessments of actual readership—that can be applied to individual works. Although "vernacular" could designate a work consumed and valued by those blacks who speak nonstandard forms of English, the term has more commonly served as a claim that a work, irrespective of its popularity, displays the formal features associated with vernacular speech or sensibilities. Thus a black aesthetic critic such as Larry Neal could, in a few short years, go from proclaiming the irrelevancy of Ellison's *Invisible Man* to "contemporary Black youth" to insisting that the novel reflects a "cultural nationalism" deemed to be "operative throughout all sections of the black community" without having to adduce any changes in the novel's popularity among contemporary black youth to account for his change of mind.[35] Fiedler's analysis, in both *What Was Literature?* and *An Inadvertent Epic,* which made a case for the popular in terms of readership that includes Stowe's *Uncle Tom's Cabin,* Thomas Dixon's *The Leopard's Spots,* and Margaret Mitchell's *Gone with the Wind,* perhaps illustrates why some critics were content with merely formal invocations of "the popular." The books that a great many people like to read are not always, perhaps not often, progressive. As Wilson Moses observes in another context in addressing black literature, "There is no evidence to support the idea that cultural sympathies to mass culture lead to racial responsibility."[36] This default anti-institutional/antiestablishment posture in regard to literature sorted nicely with the overriding political stance on the black Left that had by the 1970s begun to seize upon the shortcomings of the civil rights movement to turn virtually all gains into losses by an "overstatement of the limits of the reforms associated with the prior period of civil rights activism."[37] From the standpoint of many 1970s black scholars, the orientation of *Phylon*'s "The Negro in Literature" symposium—and indeed of much of the journal's work at that time, which presumed that the pressing need for intellectual life was to fashion a cultural response to a world no longer defined by Jim Crow—was hopelessly compromised from the outset. Broadly speaking, the fact that the civil rights gains of the 1950s and 1960s did not end racial disparity, particularly at the bottom end of the economic scale, made it possible to paint the writers and critics who in the 1950s through the mid-1960s expressed optimism about the imminent collapse of racial inequality as naïve dupes of a power structure that had recognized it could seize on the putative color blindness of liberal humanism to contain demands for racial egalitarianism. From this view, while it may have been true in the past that it was the nation's failure to live up to its expressed ideals that had permitted the exclusion of blacks from full membership in the polity, it was now the case that the nation was eager to embrace those very ideals because, by definition, they excluded blacks.

Although too dismissive of the historical changes attending the demise of constitutionally sanctioned segregation, black critics of this period were not incorrect in seeing the need to challenge the "orthodox narrative that treated [1960s] reforms as tantamount to exhaustive fulfillment of the ideal of social justice."[38] Too much work remained to be done. From the standpoint of literary history, it is important to see that in making this challenge, these critics were participating in changes that were marking the term of the project of African American literature. As I suggested in the previous chapter, integral to the character of what African American literature *had been* was a prospective posture. This posture carried with it several

assumptions, the most significant being that the black literature of the past, while punctuated by some verifiable gems, did
not constitute a classic literature. The attitude of the Harlem
Renaissance's critical antennae toward much of the literature
that preceded it, and that of writers of the 1930s and 1940s to
the Harlem Renaissance itself, was angled to receive signals of
shortcomings and insufficiencies, all in service of a progressive
narrative of a literature moving toward maturity. The passage
from Blyden Jackson's 1950 *Phylon* article that serves as an epi-
graph for this chapter is illustrative. Jackson describes the "calls
to integrate the Negro into our national life" as "a sign that
both America and its Negroes are reaching a certain maturity"
and that "Negro writers are promising to do their bit in keeping
pace with the latest trend." Immaturity for Jackson was marked
by "exaggerated self-consciousness" and an unfortunate parochialism. Maturity, on the other hand, announced itself in
what Jackson saw as a growing capacity or willingness on the
part of the black writer to see the particular plight of black
Americans in relation to what was deemed the broader human
condition. In elaborating his point, Jackson writes, "Gwendolyn Brooks' *Satin-Legs Smith* represents without apology the
South Side of Chicago, but none of his unabashed local color
prevents him from representing very well also the diminution
of man as a romantic spirit in the machinemade [*sic*] monot-
ony of the modern metropolis. Redding's *Stranger and Alone* is
a study of Uncle Tomism, but a study of Uncle Tomism which
illuminates *sub specie aeternitatis* the ubiquitous errand-boys
for Caesar."[39] The clear implication is that it was only at that

moment that much of black literature had begun to leave behind a narrow commitment to the particularity of the black experience—the parochialism—that had defined the literature of the past. That this assessment is a version of the criticism that Nathan Huggins leveled at the Harlem Renaissance in his influential study of that movement, as well as a version of what Renaissance writers themselves had said about their predecessors, is precisely the point.[40] In this assessment, mature black literature, while remaining faithful to the particular expression of character type and behavior it sought to represent in black life, would consistently present black characters and their actions as members and behaviors of a group that was defined not by race but by broader swaths of human behavior and history.

To reiterate, the posture assumed by Jackson and other critics toward African American literature was prospective. "We build our temples for tomorrow" is how Langston Hughes expresses that orientation in another context, suggesting again that African American literature was more concerned with what it was going to be than with what it was already.[41] Arnold Rampersad and, before him, Nathan Huggins have pointed out that this posture seems to have entailed something of an inferiority complex about black achievement, which, as Rampersad argues, dogs even the most stunning achievements of the Harlem Renaissance. Wallace Thurman's *Infants of the Spring* is, of course, one of the earlier works structured around the theme of black artistic immaturity and naïveté. According to Huggins and Rampersad, this sense of having a literature that has not yet measured up to the appropriate standards leaves the writer unable to mine the body of work that has been most concerned with the imaginative recreation and response to the lived experience closest to her own. Rather than being able to engage the work most immediate to her own concerns, she constructs alternate, more distant, less complicated pasts on which she can draw for the guiding principle of artistic creation.[42]

This sense of inferiority could have been crippling for African American writers of this moment in terms of their relation to their white Jim Crow contemporaries (and it has indeed become the case that many critics today feel that it was), because within a social and political order predicated on black inferiority, for black writers and critics to concede that this same system had made their own literature inferior put them in a position of tutelage to white writers who should have been their peers. In fact, it could be argued that this situation defined the terms of entry into the ranks of serious criticism as an author's willingness to disparage other black writers. Black critics made their bones by taking down the work of black predecessors.

To some extent—perhaps to a great extent—this is true, and yet what prevented this posture from becoming debilitating was that for these writers the charge of immaturity and stunted or belated development was also one that they leveled against American literature in general, and southern literature in particular. It is perhaps too easy to forget how recent in historical terms was the consolidation of an American literary canon. By the 1940s and 1950s, African American writers were confronting not a long-established consensus on the enduring quality of American literature but one that was in the process of being formed. In a recent study of the institutionalization of the study of American literature, Elizabeth Renker writes, "When I interviewed Daniel Aaron and R. W. B. Lewis, prominent early scholars of American literature, I asked both in what year they thought the field had achieved institutional status. Aaron said: the 1930s; Lewis: the 1960s."[43] Ernest Hemingway, as Ralph Ellison famously reminded us, had declared all American writing before Twain's *Adventures of Huckleberry Finn* of little use for establishing the basis for a contemporary American literature.[44] And all of these writers were well aware of the censures that H. L. Mencken, in "The Sahara of the Bozart," had leveled against the cultural vacancy of southern literature.[45] If racism had hindered the development of black literature, part of the broader sense was that it had wrought similar damage on twentieth-century American literature as a whole, which was the argument that Ellison made in one of his midcentury essays.[46] White American writers' evasion of the Negro problem in the twentieth century had left their literature enervated and empty. Certainly, before his more obtuse responses to the civil rights movement in the 1950s and despite his sometimes melodramatic and problematic characterizations of black people in his fiction, William Faulkner was viewed by some black writers of the period as facing a problem similar to their own, namely building a serious literature on the basis of a society that had made such literature a difficult undertaking because writing in that society had had to serve political ends.

Another way of making this point is to say that African American literature was modernist, albeit not so much in the sense of a hyper-attentiveness to stylistic innovation but in a constant reiteration of the sense that as a writer, one operated under the imperative to "make it new."

Yet however tenable it was in the 1950s to presume the immaturity of most black literature written up to that point, the liabilities of taking this stance became more apparent over the next decade and a half, particularly as American literature emerged as a topic for study and its short history became filled up, not with a series of literary rehearsals for the main act to come (although the story told about this literature did have a narrative structure), but with a set of bona fide classics in their own right. This classic American literature, as we know, was darkened by the shadow of race as a topic and a metaphysical property but not, for the most part, by the presence of black authors themselves. Against this consolidation of American literature, to argue that black authors, by and large, had not yet produced literature was to acquiesce in their absence from the body of American literary work deemed suitable for serious study. Part of the story, then, of what African American literature was, as opposed to what it is now, has a great deal to do with the academization of the study of literature in colleges and universities.

Addison Gayle trenchantly describes this point, and the liabilities of the 1950s posture, in a 1968 essay on Herbert Hill's anthology of African American literature, *Soon One Morning: New Writing by American Negroes, 1940–1962*. Published in 1963, *Soon One Morning* featured most of the major African American literary authors of the late Jim Crow era—Langston Hughes, Richard Wright, Gwendolyn Brooks, Ralph Ellison, James Baldwin—along with essays by scholars such as Horace Cayton, J. Saunders Redding, John Hope Franklin, and St. Clair Drake. Hill introduced his anthology by celebrating the most recent black writing as marking a literary coming-of-age. Opening with a declaration that the "greater part of contemporary American writing is characterized by a determination to break through the limits of racial parochialism into the whole range of the modern writer's preoccupations," Hill ends his introduction by admonishing his reader that a "profound disservice is done to the Negro writer, now and in the future, if any criteria are invoked except those of art and literature."[47]

Disputing the terms of Hill's assessment of black literary writing, Gayle observes:

> If one pushes Hill's thesis to its logical conclusion, Negro writers are now, at long last, capable of entering the "mainstream of American Literature." The prodigal son has returned home, been scrubbed clean of the dirt and grime of protest, been baptized in the crystal clear waters of universality and, like Ralph Ellison, has "transcend[ed] the traditional preoccupations of the Negro writer; [and] ultimately . . . is concerned not with race but with man."[48]

Then using John Bunyan's *Pilgrim's Progress* to ridicule Hill's representation of African American literature as finally laboring into the Promised Land with the emergence of Baldwin and Ellison, Gayle writes:

If one believes Hill, soon one morning the society will become cognizant of the fact that Negro writers have come down from "The Hill Difficulty," journeyed through "By Pass Meadow," and around "Doubting Castle," on through "The Sea of Despond," traversing "the limits of racial parochialism into the whole range of the modern writer's preoccupations." Presumably, therefore, Negro writers will at long last be welcomed into the company of the literary host; shown their rightful seats in the academic circles; and anointed with the oils of fame, posterity, and wealth. In other words, the New Canaan lies across the road, and soon one great getting up morning, "in sandal schoon and scallop shells," Negro writers will waltz through the gilded doors which lead to American literary immortality.[49]

Against this Gayle makes two devastating points. The first is that, contrary to Hill's insistence, the works of Baldwin and Ellison are not so different from that of their black "predecessors," among whom he includes Chester Himes, Ann Petry, William Gardner Smith, and Richard Wright, as writers steeped in the protest tradition that for Hill stands in the way of producing true art. The second is that Hill's argument is based on the "untenable premise" that "Negro writers are denied entrance into Canaan because they have not met the artistic rules for entrance." Gayle continues,

> Nothing, however, could be further from the truth. To my knowledge, no critic has accused William Dean Howells of overwhelming artistic ability; none has suggested that

artistically Harriet Beecher Stowe measures up to Marcel
Proust or Henry James. And one discusses [Upton Sinclair's] *The
Jungle*, Dreiser's *Sister Carrie*, and Fitzgerald's *The Great Gatsby*
in sociological, not aesthetic, terminology. It would appear,
therefore, that Negro writers have been excluded from
contemporary American literature not because of artistic
deficiencies but primarily because of race.[50]

By which he means "racism." Accordingly, the balance of the
essay then recounts the differing responses by faculty and students at the City College of New York (CCNY) to Gayle's proposal to add Hill's anthology of Negro literature, despite its
shortcomings, to the reading list of a prebaccalaureate course
he taught in the college's SEEK program during the spring of
1967. As he recounts the incident in his autobiography, members of the college's minority faculty, which included Toni
Cade Bambara and Barbara Christian, supported his effort.[51]
The white faculty members, by Gayle's account, are almost
unanimous in their opposition, even though none of them had
read the anthology. Their stated concern is that the anthology
doesn't count as mainstream American literature and that,
because of this, the students, most of whom are either black or
Puerto Rican, will be insulted or embarrassed by being made to
read this literature. Gayle is eventually allowed to use the book,
though, and in response to the objections of his white colleagues, he administers a questionnaire to his students at the
end of the course asking such questions as whether they liked
the course, found it embarrassing, and so on. In contrast to

the faculty, the students are virtually unanimous in their admiration of the course material. They praise the anthology and recommend that it, and other texts like it, be taught in similar courses. Gayle laments, though, that despite student wishes and despite the fact that the books he champions derive from "the experiences, that life of turmoil, sorrow, joy, and confusion, so akin to Canaan's other inhabitants," African American literature will remain outside the curricula of college campuses "unless something radical happens to America's educational system."[52]

Gayle, of course, is writing on the cusp of the change that from where he sits seems at once imaginable and unimaginable. On the one hand, his presence and that of many of his students at CCNY was the result of civic and political action as well as social pressure and negotiations of the sort that had led to the passage of the 1964 Civil Rights Act and the 1965 Voting Rights Act, affirming the status of black Americans as members of the polity.[53] On the other hand, the responses of his white colleagues to his modest proposal seemed to indicate that the reorganization of American literary pedagogy was going to be a drawn-out process. Not only did Gayle not foresee that within the decade African American literature would begin to be taught on majority-white campuses across the country, albeit not necessarily or primarily in American literature classrooms, but he also did not register how imminent were some changes on his own campus. The recalcitrance of his white colleagues did not tell the entire story. White radical students from a group called the Du Bois Society demanded in the fall of 1968 that CCNY establish a "School of Black and Puerto Rican Studies."[54] Additionally, the goals of the SEEK program began to attract the support of white teachers and scholars. Feminist poet Adrienne Rich, who joined the program in 1968, speaks passionately of teaching *The Souls of Black Folk* and Richard Wright's "The Man Who Lived Underground" alongside D. H. Lawrence's *Sons and Lovers* and Plato's *Republic*.[55] On a larger scale, as Noliwe Rooks recounts in her history of the establishment of black studies programs on predominantly white campuses, the Ford Foundation, under the leadership of McGeorge Bundy, was by 1968 actively involved in supporting African American studies on college campuses around the country. According to Rooks, between 1968 and 1972, Ford Foundation grants to black studies "totaled more than ten million dollars and supported two dozen programs."[56]

But I want to draw attention to two factors that are crucial to understanding the larger point about periodization I'm making here. First, Gayle's essay underscores why the developmental narrative that was constitutive of African American literature had a specific shelf life: as American literary scholarship went from deprecating to celebrating its past achievements, to insist that Jean Toomer was inferior to F. Scott Fitzgerald was to capitulate to racism. If a developmental narrative was going to be defensible, it would have to be rewritten in such a way as to shield black literature from the charge of inferiority— and indeed that is what happened over the next two decades. To leap momentarily over the emergence of the Black Arts and Black Aesthetic Movement (in which Gayle's writing was to

prove central) in order to take up the academic criticism stem-
ming from that movement: Robert Stepto's *From behind the Veil:
A Study of Afro-American Narrative* (1979) tells a story of black
literary development in terms of the working out of an autono-
mous, self-authorizing black literary sensibility in which the
story of black literature was of a literature becoming itself and
not of a literature finally gaining admittance to the Olympian
realm where dwelt the classic texts of white authors.[57] Henry
Louis Gates Jr., in *Figures in Black: Words, Signs, and the "Racial"
Self* and *The Signifying Monkey: A Theory of African American Literary Criticism,* kept the charge of immaturity in play but leveled
it not at black literature, which he found to be a rich body of
work from its inception, but at the critical tradition itself,
which had not yet figured out how to do justice to its collective
object of inquiry. But before I take this up, there is a second
aspect of Addison Gayle's criticism of *Soon, One Morning* that
needs underscoring. Although by 1972 Gayle will declare, "The
proponents of a Black Aesthetic, the idol smashers of America,
call for a set of rules by which Black literature and art is to be
judged and evaluated," in his essay on Hill's anthology he makes
his case by invoking standards he sees as applying equally to
both American and African American writers. The problem for
Gayle at this earlier moment is not that white academics don't
know which critical standards to apply to black writing, or
that such critical standards had yet to be derived, but simply
that their prejudices prevent them from applying any standards
at all. That is, Gayle is not yet bringing to bear the kind of critique that characterizes the Black Aesthetic arguments he is

helping to shepherd in at this same time. The claim in his *Phylon* essay is not that black texts are different but that they are the same as white texts, and it is only a commitment to racism that prevents white academics from seeing this.

In a very real way Gayle is straddling the historical divide I'm sketching out here. His essay indicates that at the moment of his writing, black particularity, which was on its way to becoming the center of gravity in the project of assessing black culture and interpreting black literature, had not yet secured its status as a desideratum of black critical practice. To be sure, as I noted in the previous chapter, the imperative to account for black distinctiveness exerted a force throughout the period, but it was equally matched by claims that only prejudice made blacks different from whites. Gayle's essay, by insisting that twentieth-century black literature was as good as its white counterparts, looks both forward and backward. By insisting on a twentieth-century African American literary history as a history of achievement rather than of shortcomings, Gayle sets the stage for what will soon be a critical project preoccupied with producing new terms for the appreciation of its myriad cultural products. In "Perhaps Not So Soon One Morning," however, he merely sets that stage but does not step onto it. What holds him back is apparent in the rhetorical strategy of the essay itself: its range of allusion and points of reference are the Western literary canon, from the Bible and the *Odyssey* to Bunyan and Coleridge to James and Proust. It remains meaningful for Gayle in this essay to think of African American literature as simply an unacknowledged part of a canon whose values and standards can be applied universally.

To draw a contrast between his moment and ours, it seems, if anything, a little harder to say something like that now—at least not without qualification. But this difference makes it a little clearer for us to see what African American literature was— which was a literature in which claiming to be *different from* and claiming to be *the same as* the dominant society could appear to have equal critical force.

3

The Future of the Past

At any given moment in academic discourse there are some writers whose epigrammatic style proves virtually irresistible to scholars across a range of disciplines—writers whose words seem at once to sum up our most pressing concerns and to defy precise paraphrase, leaving one unsure whether they have expertly condensed the problems of the moment or merely achieved a vague evocativeness that serves to cover a variety of sins. Walter Benjamin has been one such figure of late, and his "Theses on the Philosophy of History" one such text. The particular thesis I have in mind is thesis VI, which reads:

> To articulate the past historically does not mean to recognize it "the way it really was" (Ranke). It means to seize hold of a memory as it flashes up at a moment of danger. Historical materialism wishes to retain that image of the past which unexpectedly appears to man singled out by history at a moment of danger. The danger affects both the content of the tradition and its receivers. The same threat hangs over

both: that of becoming a tool of the ruling classes. In every era the attempt must be made anew to wrest tradition away from a conformism that is about to overpower it. The Messiah comes not only as the redeemer; he comes as the subduer of Antichrist. Only that historian will have the gift of fanning the spark of hope in the past who is firmly convinced that even the dead will not be safe from the enemy if he wins. And this enemy has not ceased to be victorious.[1]

What makes these words especially attractive is that they posit a dynamic relation between past and present that almost obliterates history, thereby casting the present-day historian in the role of potential hero, or even freedom fighter, on behalf of a past that almost magically becomes our contemporary in terms of what it needs or demands from us.

What these words raise with a vengeance is the question of our responsibility to the past, not merely in terms of getting it right but also in terms of whether or not there is such a thing as "getting it right" outside of a struggle for justice. One recent Benjamin-inflected history that raises these and other questions is Ian Baucom's *Specters of the Atlantic: Finance Capital, Slavery, and the Philosophy of History,* a book organized around the incident of the slave ship *Zong* in 1781 in which 132 captives were thrown overboard—which is to say, murdered—in order to make possible a recovery of investment from the ship's insurers. This incident is famously represented in J. M. W. Turner's painting, *Slave Ship* or *Slavers Throwing Overboard the Dead and Dying—Typhoon Coming On,* and more recently, in Fred D'Aguiar's lesser-known novel,

Feeding the Ghosts. Baucom argues that the *Zong* horror was enabled by a system dependent on the idea that it is possible to
compensate individuals for losses incurred through enterprise
undertaken for profit. That is, finance capital depends on insurance, which assumes that by substituting or exchanging one
thing for another it is possible to redeem losses and to make
someone whole again. In Baucom's account because it was this
system of exchange that underwrote the injustice done to the
victims of the *Zong,* we must instead investigate what it might
mean to do justice to those victims without playing by the rules
of exchange. Can there be an alternate way of giving value to the
lives of those who were unceremoniously murdered at sea?
Against this history, Baucom wants to "discuss a discourse in
which the theory of value upon which a politics of diasporic re-
membrance founds itself originates in a refusal to identify either value or justice with that law of exchange which was the
true law governing the outcome of the *Zong* trials." (It should be
noted that central to Baucom's concern with the *Zong* trials is
that, despite the effort of abolitionists to use the murder of the
captives as a showcase to indict slavery, the case turned on
whether or not the insurance company was obliged "to compensate the shipowners for their loss.") For Baucom it is not enough
to recognize slavery as part of an unjust past, because even to
acquiesce in seeing the past as past is to make such crimes as
that committed in 1781 "only an occasion for sympathy and a
decent burial (of the dead, of the slave trade) that the living
might live on unhaunted by these specters of the Atlantic."
Against this understanding of time structured by clear

demarcations between past and present, and in order to allow our present to be haunted by the past, Baucom urges us "to acknowledge the unevenness of time, the uncanny, repetitive presentness of the past within the present," and to recognize "the endless temporal exchanges of a heterochronic modernity, a modernity, in Benjamin's words, in which our 'now being' is 'charged to the bursting point with time,' a modernity in which, as [Paul] Gilroy has it, one of the greatest challenges available to us is the challenge of learning what it means to live nonsynchronously." In sum, Baucom asserts, "Time does not pass, it accumulates," and we must therefore see our time and the time of the *Zong* as one, as part of one long twentieth century.[2]

My purpose in describing, I hope accurately, Baucom's argument here is not only to draw attention to its view of "history"— one that seems much grander and more elaborately theorized than the comparatively mundane insistence on history I am making here—but also to highlight the way that the recent recourse to history in discussions of African American life and culture has tended to make discrete periodizations beside the point, and to attach a taint of injustice to periodization itself, which by its very definition has to be concerned as much with discontinuity as continuity and has to insist on some distinction between past and present. Accordingly, to proclaim the "was-ness" of something so recent as the last century of African American literary production carries with it an almost sinister cast. Nonetheless, at the risk of courting the sinister, it is my contention here that to understand both past and present, we have to put the past behind us.

Similar to the way that the "research stimulated by the black politics of the 1960s" made black and African American history "more widely known and better documented" than ever before, recent scholarship oriented by diasporic, transatlantic, and slave-era concerns has further opened the past to scholarly inquiry.[3] But also like that earlier wave of inquiry, which produced "gaps" in understanding as a result of its concentration "on seeking historical antecedents for the culture and politics of the 1960s,"[4] this recent wave of scholarship has suffered from blind spots as it has sought to contest what the historian Nikhil Singh describes as "the rise of . . . color-blind universalism" in the present.[5] Just as the post-1960s generation of African Americanist inquiry "narrowed . . . the study of politics . . . to men and movements seeking purely racial goals," the most recent generation of scholarship, while seemingly opening up black concerns by casting them, à la Baucom and so many others, as centrally engaged with the philosophical and legal foundations of the West, has, like its post-1960s counterpart, "frequently limited [its analyses] to one oversimplified explanation—racism."[6] That is, the "discovery" made again and again by recent scholarship is that despite news to the contrary, "racism" still exists. At issue here is not the fact that some people—maybe a significant number of people—still harbor some array of stereotypes and phobias about people from other groups. Rather, what needs getting at is what follows when the problem of racism has become a problem of history. For once racism is described as a problem of how we understand and acknowledge the power of history, "color blindness" becomes something other than pretending not to notice conventional marks of racial difference even as one makes important decisions based on that difference. Rather, "color blindness" turns out to be a kind of blindness to the presentness of the past, a refusal to see that people can still be victimized by the past, and that the past can be victimized by the present.

To risk an overstatement, much of what purports to be progressive racial scholarship and racial literature, whether it invokes the horrors of the slave era, the Middle Passage, or the ongoing impoverishment of black urban communities, can be seen as oriented rhetorically toward making clear to a nonreceptive audience that includes the likes of the current Supreme Court majority, a very vocal cadre of white and black conservatives, and people like Bill Cosby that racism—which is to say, the history of racial trauma—still matters and still explains ongoing inequalities. Accordingly, race, or antiracism, must remain an integral part of the way we respond to the world and contest the status quo. On this view the abolitionist and civil rights movements stand out as commitments to social justice that can serve as repositories or inspirational examples of how we might in the present confront the emergency represented by the ongoing inequalities of our own times. As Singh puts it, what we will thankfully discover upon viewing properly the "long history" of the civil rights movement is that black activists and intellectuals "left behind a rich legacy of radical visions for imagining coalitions and thinking and feeling beyond the nation state" that has currently tossed its color-blind veil over the face of injustice.[7] As indicated by the title of Singh's book, *Black Is a Country: Race and the Unfinished Struggle for*

Democracy, viewing the past in this way also argues for an ongoing intellectual and political imperative to discern and assert a basis for black solidarity at a moment when it appears that the obvious intellectual and political justifications supporting this claim have otherwise eroded. Or to quote Tommie Shelby, a political philosopher who shares much of Singh's outlook, "a theoretically coherent and practically feasible black political solidarity can and should be maintained" until we achieve social justice, at which point it will be "no longer necessary for those who are dark to think of themselves as an independent political unit."[8]

The calls for a "renewal" of black solidarity in the late twentieth and early twenty-first century by scholars such as Singh and Shelby can be taken as a bleak rejoinder to one of the questions posed by Hill and Holman in *Phylon* in 1950: If the dream of a future unmarked by racial difference as a measure of civic worth has finally become politically viable, it is only because such a dream now serves as an updated version of the "thin disguise" of equality that the U.S. Supreme Court in *Plessy v. Ferguson* (1896) had draped over white supremacy at the dawn of the Jim Crow era. "Thin disguise" is, of course, the term used by Justice Harlan in his dissent in *Plessy,* deriding the court majority's pretense that "separate but equal" was anything more than an attempt to realign the Constitution with white social dominance. Accordingly, if the politics of the Right at the current moment entails a pursuit of white supremacy by means less obvious than Jim Crow but nonetheless as powerful, then the struggle against white supremacy must continue, and there would be every reason to expect African American literature to retain its indexical and instrumental relations to the struggle against that order.

In Singh's view, however, the continuity of the past with the present has become obscured because conservative and liberal elements have conspired to produce an account of the civil rights era in which its goals and scope have been narrowed to focus solely on ending racism within the U.S. nation-state. According to Singh, the U.S. Supreme Court has been a chief proponent of this version of the past, with the result that "The prevailing common sense of the post–civil rights era is that race is the provenance of an unjust, irrational ascription and prejudice, while nation is the necessary horizon of our hopes for color-blind justice, equality, and fair play."[9] Singh argues that, as a consequence, taking race into account in order to pursue social justice has been proscribed by the current judicial regime for whom "race now means racism, especially when it is used to define or defend the interests of a minority community."[10]

If the *Plessy* case marks the beginning of the Jim Crow era, which produced the conditions necessary for the emergence of African American literature; and if the test cases that led to *Brown v. Board of Education* signaled the beginning of the end for legalized segregation, thus helping to illuminate the reality that from its inception African American literature had been committed to undermining the conditions that brought it into being; then the U.S. Supreme Court decisions in *Grutter v. Bollinger* and *Gratz v. Bollinger*, commonly known as the Michigan cases (to which we can add the Court's 2007 ruling in *Parents Involved in Community Schools v. Seattle School District No. 1*), provide a vantage point from which to see what has happened—and what is happening—to writing by black Americans now that African American literature has come to an end.

The Michigan cases and *Parents Involved in Community Schools v. Seattle School District No. 1,* respectively, addressed whether race could legitimately be considered a factor in making admissions decisions at colleges and professional schools for the purpose of achieving diversity and in assigning pupils to primary and secondary schools for the purpose of desegregation. By a narrow majority in the Michigan Law School case, the Court did not fully banish consideration of race for admissions but instead concluded that the Fourteenth Amendment's "Equal Protection Clause does not prohibit the Law School's narrowly tailored use of race in admissions decisions to further a compelling interest in obtaining the educational benefits that flow from a diverse student body." (The Seattle and Kentucky school districts in *Parents Involved in Community Schools* did not fare as well: Their pupil assignment policies were declared unconstitutional.) Yet even the Michigan ruling in favor of a narrow use of race in educational settings was tenuous. Justice Sandra Day O'Connor's majority opinion made it clear that race was on a short lease, writing, "We expect that 25 years from now, the use of racial preferences will no longer be necessary to further the interest approved."[11] Although O'Connor did not elaborate the reasons for putting these remedies on the clock, in the view of critics like Singh, even this quarter-century reprieve for race-conscious public policy was problematic because it presumed a color-blind future in defiance of "the political lesson of the long civil rights era ... that we advance equality only by continually passing through a politics of race and by refusing the notion of a definitive 'beyond' race."[12]

Given that the spate of cases challenging the use of race-conscious decision making at all levels of the nation's educational system was in large part a result of an orchestrated effort to build support for the cultural agenda of the political Right,[13] Singh's insistence on hanging on to race would appear to make a great deal of sense, particularly when the Right gleefully enlists into its cause arguments and conclusions that proved instrumental in winning progressive victories in the past (notwithstanding how compromised these victories may have been). For example, Justice Clarence Thomas, in his concurring opinion in the Seattle case, explicitly aligned his reasoning with that of the *Brown* decision, writing: "What was wrong in 1954 cannot be right today.... The plans before us base school assignment decisions on students' race. Because 'our Constitution is colorblind, and neither knows nor tolerates classes among citizens', such race-based decisionmaking [sic] is unconstitutional."[14] Against such reasoning, which might be deemed a striking example of using history as a tool of the ruling class, it would seem more than pertinent to invoke Singh's longer history of the civil rights movement.

Oddly enough, however, the difference between Singh's black radicalism and Thomas's conservative, strict constructionism may be less marked than appears to be the case at first glance. That is, Singh's conviction that black struggle gets shortchanged when it is funneled through reforming the nation-state serves as an unwitting corollary to Thomas's insistence on a color-blind Constitution. In his *Seattle* concurring opinion, Thomas acknowledges that race, in the form of racial imbalance as opposed to de jure racial segregation, will remain an ongoing feature of U.S. social life. He writes, "Unlike *de jure* segregation, there is no ultimate remedy for racial imbalance. Individual schools will fall in and out of balance in the natural course, and the appropriate balance itself will shift with a school district's changing demographics."[15] In distinguishing race from segregation, the latter of which he defines as state-sanctioned separation of races, Thomas allows for the ongoing salience of race in U.S. lived experience. Contra to what is usually alleged of advocates of color blindness, Thomas explicitly does not make "race" equivalent to "racism"—except in those instances when the state attempts to assert its authority regarding racial distinction, a distinction that inadvertently sorts well with Singh's belief that "Efforts to write racially excluded populations into national histories reinforce the false idea that the nation-state is the sole arbiter of universal values and legitimate political aims."[16] Both men want to dislodge the constitutional apparatus of the nation-state as the frame for addressing racial inequality, and both men also see racial inequality as distinct from a desire to maintain the salience of racial groups. In critiquing civil rights orthodoxy from what seem to be opposed angles, Singh and Thomas end up arguing for preserving the efficacy of black collective action, which for Thomas emerges explicitly as a return to black self-help. In fact, he introduces his dissenting opinion in *Grutter* with a little historicism of his own, quoting from Frederick Douglass's "What the Black Man Wants: An Address Delivered in Boston, Massachusetts, on 26 January 1865," and concluding, "Like Douglass, I believe blacks can achieve in every avenue of American life without the meddling of university administrators."[17] Also like Singh, Thomas is far from persuaded that racism is a thing of the past. His concurring opinion in *Grutter* asks, "Can we really be sure that the racial theories that motivated *Dred Scott* and *Plessy* are a relic of the past or that future theories will be nothing but beneficent and progressive? That is a gamble I am unwilling to take, and it is one the Constitution does not allow."[18] Like Singh and Baucom, Thomas is fighting the ghosts of history.

It is not merely argumentative sleight of hand to put two men of such obviously opposed politics on the same side of the ledger when it comes to race and the state. To be sure, Thomas and Singh are not the same, but my point is that Thomas does not need to be convinced that racism still exists in the way that Singh's argument presumes. Nor does Thomas need to be convinced that our society is not color-blind, which is another of Singh's points. Rather, Thomas readily agrees that race still does and will likely continue to matter in American social life and that we must continue to fight racism. His claim, even if we see it as malicious or misguided, is that while our society is not color-blind, our Constitution, for the good of all, is or must be so. That is, albeit for different reasons, Thomas agrees with Singh that while racial inequities continue to plague our society, to make the Constitution the primary arena for achieving social justice is the wrong way to go. The bottom line here is that notwithstanding claims to the contrary, there is nothing particularly radical in insisting that race continues to matter in U.S. social life.

Importantly, however, in closing the distance between Singh and Thomas, I have not yet adequately addressed the fact that Singh's goal in taking the longer view of the civil rights movement is to remind us that the political vision of many black writers and activists in the 1930s and 1940s did not stop at reforming the racial laws and codes of the United States but also embraced forms of radicalism that Thomas and his ilk would find inimical. Indeed, Singh and a number of other scholars have reminded us that many black writers and scholars were actively involved in international Marxist, Pan-Africanist, and decolonizing movements, the influence of which on domestic black politics was diminished in the late 1940s and early 1950s by the Myrdal consensus, McCarthyism, the cold war, and the bourgeoisification of formerly black radical thinkers.[19] Key to Singh's analysis is his observation that W. E. B. Du Bois held fast to the belief that a "transnational project for social reconstruction" must begin "with the recognition of black cohesiveness independent of other communities," even as many of his counterparts in the 1930s and 1940s began to argue that recent social changes were "initiating a process that would equalize black status within the nation state as a result of the entry (or integration) of blacks into civic institutions."[20] For Singh, it is Du Bois's steadfastness and foresight in insisting on the efficacy of "black cohesiveness" that makes his thinking diagnostic for the early twenty-first century.

As we have seen in the previous chapter, however, Du Bois's reflections on racial injustice in the 1940s assumed that the world of constitutionally sanctioned Jim Crow would persist virtually unchanged perhaps for the rest of the twentieth century. To be sure, when he struggles in *Dusk of Dawn* to explain the concept of race that "has so changed and presented so much of contradiction" that it now "constitutes a tie which I can feel better than I can explain," he finally hits on an explanation that reaches across the globe and several millennia:

> But one thing is sure and that is the fact that since the fifteenth century these ancestors of mine and their other descendants have had a common history; suffered a common disaster and have one long memory. The actual ties of heritage between the individuals of this group vary with the ancestors that they have in common and many others: Europeans and Semites, perhaps Mongolians, certainly American Indians. But the physical bond is least and the badge of color relatively unimportant save as a badge; the real essence of this kinship is its social heritage of slavery; the discrimination and insult; and this heritage binds together not simply the children of Africa, but extends through yellow Asia and into the South Seas. It is this unity that draws me to Africa.[21]

This is the broad history—reaching back in time to slavery and across space to colonized peoples around the globe—with which Du Bois and a variety of recent scholars influenced by him seek to animate and reanimate a political struggle that perpetually seems in danger of falling prey to the belief that its struggles are bound by the goal of reforming existing nation states.

Yet, as evocative as Du Bois's formulation of worldwide black identity is, *Dusk of Dawn,* on its own account, remains a Jim Crow document, premised on the belief that legalized segregation would enjoy a longer life than it did and that, consequently, black political, intellectual, and cultural activity would have to remain organized against it. So notwithstanding the poetic language with which Du Bois tries to nail down just what it is that gives race its binding power at the midpoint of the twentieth century, his language becomes more prosaic and domestic when he is ultimately pushed in *Dusk of Dawn* to answer the question "But what is this group; and how do you differentiate it; and how can you call it 'black' when you admit it is not black?" In response Du Bois writes: "I recognize it quite easily and with full legal sanction; the black man is a person who must ride 'Jim Crow' in Georgia."[22]

If one were to take this as Du Bois's last word on racial identity and then do him the courtesy of taking him at his word, then one would also have to say that at present, since there is no one who must ride Jim Crow in Georgia, there are no longer any black men in Georgia or anywhere else in the United States—at least, not on the terms of identification that Du Bois provides here. There are, however, plenty of people who cannot afford to ride first class in Georgia or in Illinois or in California, or who cannot afford the price of any ticket whatsoever,

and while for some of them, the story of their current impoverishment can be narrated as a tale beginning with the capture
and enslavement of their ancestors, for others such a tale is not
possible, although their impoverishment is equally real.

Of course, it would be silly and unhelpful to claim that black
people somehow disappeared with the demise of Jim Crow or
that the beliefs and attitudes that sustained segregation have
disappeared as well. In truth, Du Bois's sharp retort to his white
interlocutor is ironic: if whites were truly as incredulous about
the reality of race as the question put to him implies they are,
there could be no Jim Crow in the south. Nonetheless, from the
standpoint of thinking about literary production, *Dusk of Dawn*
reminds us that the literature of its moment was oriented by the
effort to change or repeal the laws that significantly shaped black
social and political life from the 1890s through the 1960s. By contrast, contemporary black political and cultural inquiry, by its
own admission, is not similarly oriented.

So while a desire for historical accuracy partially motivates
attempts to ground African American literary practice in a terrain more expansive than the world of Jim Crow, one can also
see how proving such a claim would be an existential necessity.
In a society that no longer sanctions Jim Crow, there could not
be a literature structured by its imperatives. When racial identity can no longer be law, it must become either history or
memory—that is, it must be either what some people once were
but that we no longer are, or the way we were once upon a time,
which still informs the way we are. If a Du Bois can no longer
give the sharp "Jim Crow" retort to the question of what defines

blacks as a group, then what remains is that "long memory" of a "common disaster" and a "heritage of slavery . . . discrimination and insult" to bind our people together. To make a poet black (to paraphrase Countee Cullen) is to bid her sing her past as her identity.

Walter Benn Michaels has helpfully delineated the way that identity and memory inform each other through what he calls "historicism"—the process by which *the past* (what happened) becomes *our past* (what happened to us)—in American literature of the late twentieth century. Michaels writes,

> Without the idea of a history that is remembered or forgotten (not merely learned or unlearned), the events of the past can have only a limited relevance to the present, providing us at best with causal accounts of how things have come to be the way they are, at worst with objects of antiquarian interest. It is only when it's reimagined as the fabric of our own experience that the past can be deployed in the constitution of identity and that any history can properly become ours.[23]

In Michaels's analysis, Toni Morrison's *Beloved* (1987) provides the "definitive articulation" of historicism.[24] Her concept of "rememory," which Sethe, the novel's main character, explains to her daughter, Denver, is the way that "What I remember is a picture floating around out there outside my head. I mean, even if I don't think it, even if I die, the picture of what I did, or knew, or saw is still out there. Right in the place where it happened." And in response to Denver's question—"Can other people see it?"—Sethe says, "The picture is still there and what's more, if you go there—you who never was there—if you go there and stand in the place where it was, it will happen again; it will be there for you, waiting for you."[25] What "rememory" performs within the space of the novel, *Beloved* as a novel performs for its readers, which is to redescribe "something we have never known as something we have forgotten and thus makes the historical past a part of our own experience."[26]

A similar project drives David Bradley's novel *The Chaneysville Incident*, published six years before *Beloved*. If one is at all unclear about the difference between "history" and "historicism," *The Chaneysville Incident* dramatizes the contrast by making its protagonist, John Washington, a historian. The tale itself, set in the late twentieth century, is an attempt to piece together the narrative of the fate of a band of nineteenth-century runaway slaves—a story involving John's grandfather, CK Washington, as well as his father, Moses Washington.

Toward the end of that novel, after trying fruitlessly to figure out what happened to the runaways, John is ready to admit the limitations of the historical method and give up the attempt. But when he tells his white girlfriend, Judith, that he is ready to stop trying, she responds by chastising him as a

hot-stuff historian, superscholar, able to leap to conclusions in a single bound . . . [and] make a bonfire by rubbing two dry facts together, so long as you're talking about the Punic Wars and Saint Francis of Assisi, or the Lost Chord and Jesus Christ. But let you come within twenty miles of where you live and it all goes out the window.

John responds initially by saying that the fault lies not in his lack of ability but in the lack of a sufficient archive. He tells Judith, "Don't you understand? There aren't any facts. All that about the runaway slaves and Moses Washington, that's extrapolation. It's not facts. I've used the facts." Unimpressed, Judith urges him to "get more facts." And when he complains again that "There *aren't* any more facts," she tells him, significantly, "Then forget the facts."[27]

And forget he does—after a fashion. Fueled by alcohol and guided by the voice of Old Jack, a recently deceased crony of his father's, John is able to "hear" and retell the story of the runaways—a story that the novel requires we take as the truth— and in which the cornered runaways commit suicide rather than submit to reenslavement, secure in the knowledge that "when the Stillness came upon them they would simply go away and live in a place where there were no men with pale skins who stole the spirit by telling lies."[28]

John then enacts his own belief in the truth of his recreated narrative by setting up his own immolation as a historian and as a person. He writes:

Then I gathered up the tools of my trade, the pens and inks and pencils, the pads and the cards, and carried them out into the clearing. I kicked a clear space in the snow and set them down, and over them I built a small edifice of kindling, and then a frame of wood. I went back inside the cabin and got the kerosene and brought it back and poured it freely over the pyre, making sure to soak the cards thoroughly.[29]

He ignites the pyre, and the story ends with John wondering whether Judith will understand the meaning of what he is doing, leaving us to presume that he, like his father before him and like the runaways before them, has chosen to return home.[30] Importantly, this holocaust of history, which confirms John's belief in the story that he has recreated, finds its origin in a history of the slave trade that Bradley places at the center of the novel. Here, John Washington remarks that

> IN THE YEAR OF OUR LORD 1441, a Portuguese sailing captain named Antam Goncalvez permitted a certain light-skinned Moorish gentleman, who was then enjoying the captain's hospitality, to ransom himself and two young male companions at the expense of ten dark-skinned gentlemen and gentlewomen from the sub-Sahara. This incident marks the beginning of the phenomenon known as the African Slave Trade.

Washington then goes on to recite the numbers and the history of the slave trade, intoning the litany of its atrocities, only to assert finally that even so "knowledgeable a historian probably does not understand the African Slave Trade—certainly does not understand it if he is white."[31]

Although the novel will subsequently qualify John's assertion that whites cannot understand the past of the slave trade in the way that blacks do, *The Chaneysville Incident* does view black identity as a way of keeping the past alive in the present. The connection between past and present is not perfect. John admits that the past may not be fully available even to blacks because "we have lost some of our belief and so we cannot *see* our ancestors." Even so, he argues:

> Africa is [not] lost to us—it is not. It cannot be. The Africanisms—the anthropologists aptly call them "survivals"—exist in all of us, independent of our knowledge or our volition. Those of us who have learned about them can recognize them in our own behavior; those of us who were raised under conditions that reinforced the behavior see it in everything we do. Those of us who know less about Africa than did the European slavers nevertheless tell tales that echo African tales, and sing songs that call on African patterns; nobody may know that the form is called "call and response," but that's the way you sing a song. And no matter how light-skinned and Episcopalian a black person is, he or she will never tell you that a person has died. "Passed away," perhaps. Or "gone home." But never died.[32]

Washington draws on the vein of historical scholarship deriving from Melville Herskovits's *The Myth of the Negro Past* (1941), which accentuates "the survivals of African traditions, attitudes, and institutionalized forms of behavior actually to be observed in present-day Negro life in the New World, particularly in the United States."[33] Yet, though Washington asserts these survivals as rationally verifiable facts, his goal here remains that of announcing the supersession of historical verification by belief: "a heritage is something you believe in. One cannot become a believer by knowing facts or even by changing one's name, wearing a dashiki, and making a pilgrimage to the Guinea Coast."[34]

According to Bradley's novel, the pathway to truth cannot be found by sifting through facts or demarcating distinctions of time and place. John Washington cannot finish the story so long as he persists in thinking like a historian. The lesson of the narrative is that truth, in the final instance, demands belief, a belief that enables one to experience death as a passing and to hear songs born on the wind.

The future of this past, at least as it is represented in these novels, is one that depends on collecting stories and memorializing events in a way that turns them into phenomena we must reexperience in order to understand. In some respects, this literature seeks to politicize a melancholy truth about the human condition, namely that, for most of us, our lives and what they meant to us are destined to be forgotten by the living. What makes this common fate flash up in this fiction as the worst fate imaginable, and one to be fought against, is that the wanton slaughter represented by the slave trade, the inhuman dumping of bodies overboard from the deck of the *Zong* is also a slaughter of identities, or as Michaels terms it, "a crime of identity."[35] Consequently, it becomes imperative in a novel like *The Chaneysville Incident* or Fred D'Aguiar's *Feeding the Ghosts* to imagine the recovery of these lost stories. As mentioned earlier, D'Aguiar's novel takes up the crimes committed on the *Zong*. In this novel, D'Aguiar attempts to create the possibility of remembering its victims by inventing a character, Mintah, who takes it upon herself to memorialize the captives before they are killed. As one woman is being dragged to the railing, Mintah calls out to her:

"Your name! What is your name?" Mintah shouted in the three languages she knew.

"Why? How will it save me?"

The woman's grip was loosened by the struggle and by another man beating her arms with his club.

"I will remember you! Others will remember you!"

And before the woman is tossed overboard, she cries out, "I am Ama!"[36]

Although in the novel Mintah's effort to write the names of the victims into history fails because the book she writes is suppressed from the trial and itself lost, the loss is in a way both fortunate and inevitable, as it leaves work for the novel to do. According to the logic D'Aguiar employs to account for the advent of his story ("the *Zong* found me"), it is the past's demand for its history that prompts the telling of this narrative.[37] That is, had the story already been committed to the historical record, there would be no need for D'Aguiar's novel. Although Mintah's book disappears, *Feeding the Ghosts* gives us Ama's name.

These fictions are defined by their commitment to making the past present to us by any representational means necessary, whether through *Beloved*'s rememories; the voice and vision of the African father in Caryl Phillips's *Crossing the River* (1997), who sets the novel in motion by selling his children but ends it by recuperating them across space and time;[38] or the two magical tapestry maps by Alice Night described in a letter at the conclusion of Edward P. Jones's novel *The Known World*, which deals with the difficult topic of blacks who owned and were owned by other blacks. The political and analytic difficulty presented by this novel, and indeed presented by various aspects of all the books mentioned here, is that they suggest that the very condition, black chattel slavery, that should have made overwhelmingly apparent the need for black solidarity could yet produce those for whom race membership did not override other motives or rationalizations. Yet despite the difficulty represented by that topic and its strong suggestion that there is no given interest that binds all black people as black people, *The Known World* is a novel that concludes with a vision of artistic unity that betokens racial unity in the form of the two maps created by Alice Night, a slave who is presumed throughout the novel to be crazy but who turns out by the end to be a representative of the artist himself. Upon seeing Alice's tapestry, one of the characters, Calvin, writes to his sister, Caldonia, the widow of the slave-owning Henry Townsend, to tell her of this marvel. He describes Alice's

> *enormous wall hanging, a grand piece of art that is part tapestry, part painting, and part clay structure—all in one exquisite Creation, hanging silent and yet songful on the Eastern wall. It is, my Dear Caldonia, a kind of map of life of the County of Manchester, Virginia. But a "map" is such a poor word for such a wondrous thing. It is a map of life made with every kind of art man has ever thought to represent himself. Yes, clay. Yes, paint. Yes, cloth. There are no people on this "map," just all the houses and barns and roads and cemeteries and wells in our Manchester. It is what God sees when He looks down*

on Manchester. At the bottom right-hand corner of this Creation there were but two stitched words, Alice Night.[39]

This is a comprehensive image conveyed through every means available to the arts of representation, as if to suggest that by employing every possible means of representation, one just might be able to get all the past within the frame. Missing from this tapestry, however, are the people of Manchester. But this is not an oversight. People do appear in another tapestry, also of Alice's creation, which as it turns out is a detail drawn from the first map and which "may well be even more miraculous than the one of the County":

> *This one is about your home, Caldonia. It is your plantation, and again, it is what God sees when He looks down. There is nothing missing, not a cabin, not a barn, not a chicken, not a horse. Not a single person is missing I suspect that if I were to count the blades of grass, the number would be correct as it was once when the creator of this work knew that world. And again, in the bottom right-hand corner are the stitched words "Alice Night."*[40]

The vision of history with which the novel concludes is one of recollection, which also becomes one of resurrection, as the dead are pictured standing outside their graves. The slave cemetery has been emptied—and even the slave-owning Henry stands beside his grave, although that "grave is covered with flowers as though he is still in it."[41]

So complete is the recollection that it extends to Calvin's individual memory. He tells Caldonia, *"There are matters in my*

memory that I did not know were there until I saw them on that wall."
But this artistic recreation of the whole of the past is a double-
edged sword for Calvin, who also owned slaves. The possibility
of complete recollection means that his crime may forever be
present, and *"that they would remember my history, that I, no matter
what I said to the contrary, owned people of our Race. I feared that they
would send me away, and even as I write you now, I am still afraid."*[42]
Whatever else it does, Calvin's fear illuminates the goal of this
fiction as that of creating a future for the past by recollecting
the black community as a whole bound by the mystic chords
of memory. Calvin's crime is not only that he enslaved someone, but also that he enslaved "people of our own race"—an
act that would seem to indicate on his part a profound lack of
racial identification. But although Calvin fears he will be exiled for his crime, there is no hint that Alice Night is considering expunging him from her tapestry. Every single person is
there. Calvin has a place in the tapestry because of who he is,
so that what he has done, and will in some sense always have
done, is of secondary importance. His is a crime that will be
indelible, but equally indelible is his race and his standing as
a member of that community. For Calvin, to have a past is to
have a race.

This dream of unity and recollection is not exclusive to the
writing by black Americans published in the aftermath of the
black literary project. As Michaels demonstrates, this sort of
writing emerges as a cultural dominant in the 1980s and 1990s
in a variety of texts taking up, respectively, the Holocaust, geno-
cide committed against American Indians, and the purported

threat to American national identity posed by so-called ethnic balkanization. For a group of writers as varied as Morrison, Leslie Marmon Silko, Stephen Greenblatt (a literary historian), and Arthur Schlesinger Jr., the pressing problem of the moment becomes that of making sure that people have the proper identities.[43] One could almost say that once it no longer became necessary for black writers to consider contesting Jim Crow as the point of their efforts, they were freed to become exclusively involved with the problem of identity. But inasmuch as the literature of identity encompasses a range of writers of different races and backgrounds, one could also say, paradoxically, that literature of identity, rather than African American literature, names the writing of the present moment.

It might appear to be a telling objection against this claim to note that a preoccupation with identity surfaces as well in African American literature, flitting across the pages of Frances Harper, Du Bois, Langston Hughes, and Zora Neale Hurston, and on and on. Those characters in Jessie Fauset's or Nella Larsen's novels who are phenotypically able to pass but are nonetheless irresistibly drawn back within the boundaries of the race stand as testaments to this urge. If scholars like Singh find discourses of black unity in the literature of the past, it is not because they have merely projected present concerns onto past actors. The desire for black unity does form a line of continuity from our historical moment to the one that preceded it. Yet it is, paradoxically, along this line of continuity that the difference between then and now shines out so clearly.

From the outset, African American literature, like all literatures, was overwhelmingly the product of an elite for whom the
connection with a broader public was less than given. In the
same way that William Dean Howells wrestled with the question of whether or not the American writer was of the masses
or of the classes,[44] black writers have had to contend with the
question of whose interests beyond their own they served. Indeed, whether in literary text or political essay, early arguments
against Jim Crow often turned on what seemed to be the pat-
ent absurdity of imposing the same classifications and restric-
tions on an illiterate field hand and an accomplished doctor of
medicine. The reader of Charles Chesnutt's novel *The Marrow of
Tradition* (1901) is supposed to feel acutely the creaturely discomfort experienced by the novel's protagonist, Dr. Miller, as
he is forced to share a railway car with sweating farm laborers.
Yet however real Miller's distaste for having to countenance
poorer blacks as social equals—and regardless that one would
have to imagine that in the social order Dr. Miller would impose
were his views to prevail, he would not have to share a car with
his malodorous fellow blacks—he is recognized in the novel, and
by the novel's working-class black characters, as the obvious
leader for their fight against injustice. Although Miller refuses
when asked to lead the men in defense of his hospital, his refusal does not stem from any sense that their fight is not his
fight, but from a calculation that armed resistance will be tantamount to suicide.[11]

Even when African American writers championed the popular idioms of the working classes in defiance of the norms of

the "smug Negro middle class," as did Langston Hughes in "The Negro Artist and the Racial Mountain," they did not necessarily do so with the expectation of currying favor with a black popular audience, as indicated by Hughes's avowal that if "colored people are pleased we are glad. If they are not, their displeasure doesn't matter either."[45] In fact, in his first autobiography, *The Big Sea* (1940), Hughes famously disparages the idea that literature produced by black elites had anything to do with the everyday lives of regular Harlemites in the 1920s. Lampooning his colleagues among the literati for believing "the race problem had been solved through Art plus Gladys Bentley" and that "the New Negro would lead a new life from then on in green pastures of tolerance created by Countee Cullen, Ethel Waters, Claude McKay, Duke Ellington, Bojangles, and Alain Locke," Hughes went on to observe cuttingly, if somewhat disingenuously, "I don't know what made any Negroes think that except that they were mostly only intellectuals doing the thinking. The ordinary Negroes hadn't heard of the Negro Renaissance. And if they had, it hadn't raised their wages any."[46]

Yet Hughes overstates the disconnect between ordinary Negroes and intellectuals in a telling way. For although black intellectuals were pursuing what amounted to a class politics through the medium of collective race-group interest—a politics that had it succeeded on its own terms would still have left unaddressed many of the concerns of "ordinary" Negroes—what made such a politics seem plausible as a race-group enterprise was the presence of Jim Crow.[47] Given that those in favor of upholding legal segregation adduced black difference or inferiority to justify their practices, black literary production could count, indexically or instrumentally, as a blow against the segregation order regardless of the standing of this work among actual black readers and regardless of whether these readers shared the work's political vision. The extent to which it is, or is not, possible to demonstrate that black literature actually played a significant role in ushering Jim Crow law from the national scene is somewhat beside the point. The key fact is that black literature's collective social and political relevance was a function of Jim Crow and the fight against it. To insist that writing by black Americans today should count as African American literature is to take what was (even under the Jim Crow conditions that lent it plausibility) a problematic assumption of race-group interest, and to attempt to renew that assumption at a time when the grounds for asserting black identity and black solidarity are ever more tenuous.

Conspicuously absent from my argument thus far has been any discussion of the burgeoning literature in the form of both pulp fiction and black-themed drama currently being produced for a black mass or popular audience. This body of literature represents much of the fiction read by the group Hughes terms "ordinary Negroes"—readers who in all likelihood are familiar with the name of Langston Hughes and who may even own some of his work, but are more likely to buy titles by Quentin Carter, K'wan, Ronald Quincy, Vickie Stringer, Teri Woods, and Carl Weber. To the chagrin of at least one writer/critic, Nick Chiles, many of these books are marketed as African American literature. Writing for the *New York Times* in an opinion piece called "Their Eyes Were Reading Smut," Chiles recounts how his initial elation upon finding a large African American literature section in a Borders bookstore in Lithonia, Georgia, turned quickly to dismay when he actually saw what was on the shelves. Chiles writes:

> With an extra spring in my step, I walked into the "African-American Literature" section—and what I saw there thoroughly embarrassed and disgusted me.
>
> On shelf after shelf, in bookcase after bookcase, all that I could see was lurid book jackets displaying all forms of brown flesh, usually half-naked and in some erotic pose, often accompanied by guns and other symbols of criminal life. I felt as if I was walking into a pornography shop, except in this case the smut is being produced by and for my people, and it is called "literature."[48]

With a genteel recoil worthy of William Dean Howells, who more than a century earlier is likewise embarrassed when his attempt to purchase a novel for a young lady at a newsstand in a railway station confronts him with a series of book covers displaying "rather more kissing and embracing going on in colors than was quite in taste,"[49] Chiles levels an objection that, like Howells's, is at once moralistic and economic. Uncomfortable with the company his books are obliged to keep, and worried that his work will find fewer and fewer buyers among his target audience, Chiles confesses to being "ashamed and mortified to see my books sitting on the same shelves as these titles; and secondly, as someone who makes a living as a writer I felt I had no way to compete with these purveyors of crassness." As the comparison with Howells illustrates, the difficulty facing writers of "serious" literature in competing successfully in the marketplace with mass-market fiction has been a long-standing issue among middle- and high-brow writers. Likewise the inability of these writers and critics of "serious" literature to shape the taste of the readership has often been an ongoing frustration. But what's also worth drawing attention to in Chiles's complaint is his unexamined assumption that the community of black readers somehow automatically constitutes *his* audience, and that for this audience to read books like those he publishes ratifies its taste. That his audience has as yet failed to prefer his books over the "tasteless collection of pornography" crowding bookstore shelves leaves Chiles feeling "defeated, disrespected and troubled about the future of my community and my little subsection of this carnivorous, unforgiving industry."[50]

In an essay titled "What Is African-American Literature?" Gerald Early responds to Chiles with an assessment much more optimistic about the present health and future prospects of literature written by blacks, however high or low their brows might be. Acknowledging the same proliferation of "urban or street-lit" that leaves Chiles wallowing in despair, Early cites three reasons that these recent changes might be positive developments: First, the growth in black readership means that it is now viable for a black author to write exclusively for a black audience. Second, the inability of the would-be black elite to impose its tastes on this readership, which has been created largely by black-owned publishing houses, means that at long last an insurgent dream of black autonomy has emerged on the literary front and that black literature "is now, more than ever, a market-driven literature, rather than an art form patronized and promoted by cultured whites and blacks as it had been in the past." And third, this literature "no longer has to be obsessed with the burden or expectation of political protest or special pleading for the humanity of the race or the worth of its history and culture as it had to in the past."[51]

Of course, according to the account I've just given of what constitutes African American literature, if black writing is no longer expected to protest segregation or to serve as a metric in the onward advancement of the race, then it no longer exists as a literature. But before taking this up in relation to Early's argument, it will be useful to explore further the grounds of his optimism about a future for African American literature. Among other things, Early notes that the phenomenon of street literature is not without precedent. The "pimp" writings of Iceberg Slim and Donald Goines achieved popularity among nonelite readers in the 1960s and 1970s without crowding out a readership for more aesthetically ambitious work. And the way that this work reveled in flouting various social norms led some readers to find in it a "true politically dynamic 'resistance' culture." Stopping short of endorsing the "resistant" reading of this literature, Early nonetheless does credit it with having "democratized and broadened the reach and content of African-American literature" in a way that "may show the maturity, not the decline, of African-American literature."[52]

In using the word "maturity" in reference to African American literature, Early hearkens back to the already discussed critical narratives about the black literary project that were common sixty years ago. But unlike those 1950s narratives of the coming of age of black literature that gauged maturity in terms of discerning among black writers a new aesthetic sophistication, Early's narrative connects contemporary writing with what he declares to be the "oldest of all self-consciously identified ethnic minority literatures in the United States going back as far as 1774 to Phyllis [sic] Wheatley's first book of poems." He continues:

> African Americans have thought longer and harder about the importance of literature as a political and cultural tool than other ethnic minorities in the United States have. The Harlem Renaissance was a movement by blacks, helped by white patrons, to gain cultural access and respectability by producing a first-rate literature. The rise of urban lit does not repudiate the black literary past, but it does suggest other ways and means of producing black literature and other ends for it as well.[53]

Although Early's goal here is to establish continuity between past and present, he seems at first glance to have created more gulfs than bridges. His emphasis on the Harlem Renaissance's desire to produce a "first-rate literature" doesn't sort well with the qualified praise he expresses earlier about recent literature's ability to ignore the tastes of those who want high literature. Whatever else a Du Bois or a Countee Cullen might have desired for future African American literature, one imagines it would not have been books with such titles as Nikki Turner's *Forever a Hustler's Wife*. And the fact that contemporary urban lit has produced some writing that Early is prepared to declare quite good doesn't nail down the claim of continuity. Fortunately for Early, his argument doesn't stop here.

He begins the final paragraph of his essay by describing his role as editor of two annual series, *Best African American Essays* and *Best African American Fiction*. In accepting this task, Early tells us that his desire was to produce works that would have "crossover appeal to various segments of the black reading public"—indeed, he hoped to "forge a sort of marriage between various types of African-American literature." To that end he tells us that he brought in an author visibly identified with the recent boom in black popular literature, the late E. Lynn Harris, to guest edit the 2009 fiction volume. Early's intent was "to use E. Lynn Harris's reach to bring serious black literature to an audience that might not be aware of it or even desire it." Acknowledging that it's much too soon to know whether or not his shotgun marriage will produce new readers of "serious" black readers from the ranks of urban-lit fans, Early wants us to see the anthology as a straightforwardly pragmatic effort to produce an African American literature for the current moment—and perhaps for the future as well. He sees reason to believe that from the "profound segmentation" of the black audience will emerge "depth and outreach, a sort of universality, dare I say, that actually bodes well for the future of this and perhaps of all of American ethnic minority literature."[54]

Although Early's optimism places him apart from Chiles, the two arguments put forth by both men are really of a piece. Early's desire to bridge the divide between urban lit and serious lit by using the appeal of a popular author to cultivate the tastes of mass-market readers is driven by the same discomfort (in a less panicked mode) that besets Chiles. He wants the readers of urban lit to upgrade their tastes, at least on occasion, and he would very much like to find *Best African American Fiction* on the shelves alongside Nikki Turner's novels because he thinks that "good" literature has a shot with this audience, provided he can get them to pick some up. But the question summoned by both accounts is why the larger social fact that the category of literary fiction currently struggles to hold its own against mass-market fiction should strike us as a racial problem, and not fundamentally as an example of what happens when all values are subordinated to those of the market. Those of us who care generally about writing may indeed care about getting more people to read what we take to be good. But there is no broadly useful social end served by viewing contemporary black writing as a collective undertaking. Indeed, despite the best intentions of those who employ the term outside its proper historical boundaries, African American literature does little more than to summon the past as guarantor of the altruistic interests of current elites and to express this cadre's proprietary interest in the tastes and habits of the more exploited members of our society under circumstances in which the success of these elites has less and less to do with type of social change that would make a profound difference in the fortunes of those at the bottom of our socioeconomic order.

Conclusion: The Past in the Present

One does not have to look very hard in Michael Thomas's prizewinning 2007 novel *Man Gone Down* to find references to African American literary history. Early in the novel's fifth chapter, the narrator, a troubled man of black, Cherokee, and Irish ancestry, intones, "It's a strange thing to go through life as a social experiment," faintly but unmistakably echoing the opening paragraphs of W. E. B. Du Bois's *The Souls of Black Folk,* in which Du Bois tells how it feels "to be a problem" by admitting, "Being a problem is a strange experience."[1] A few pages later, the narrator repeats the allusion to Du Bois and builds on it with a slant paraphrase of Langston Hughes's poem, "The Negro Speaks of Rivers," soliloquizing:

> It's a strange thing, indeed, to go through life as a social experiment. I've been to Dublin and London, walked in tobacco and cotton fields. I've been to the Oklahoma reservation Minette [his great-great grandmother] walked away from, and I've seen the Mississippi dump into the Gulf.

And I've seen a faded rainbow, like the parabolic wake of an
arrow, shot through the center of them all.[2]

It seems easy enough to say that what such allusions do (and
both Du Bois and *The Souls of Black Folk* appear elsewhere in
the story, along with several other African American writers)
is identify Thomas's novel as a greening branch on the ever-
growing tree of African American literature, testifying to the
way the history of African American literature continues to
nourish the production of black literature at present. This being said, however, it would have been just as easy, and as justifi-
able, to begin a consideration of *Man Gone Down* by noting
its myriad references to American and world literature more
broadly: Each of the novel's four sections begins with an epi-
graph drawn from T. S. Eliot's *Four Quartets*—the first two with
quotations from "Little Gidding," and the last two with lines
from "Dry Salvages"—and sprinkled here and there throughout the text are references to St. Augustine, Shakespeare, Cer-
vantes, Chekhov, Blake, Keats, Joyce, Fitzgerald, and several
more. All in all, Thomas writes with the canon of Western literature at his fingertips, and *Man Gone Down* would not be the
novel it is absent its abundance of literary reference.

But being at home with great works of literature characterizes African American literature from its inception at the dawn
of the Jim Crow era through its fulfillment as formalized Jim
Crow succumbed to political, social, judicial, and legal pressure and assault. "I sit with Shakespeare and he winces not,"
Du Bois declares in *The Souls of Black Folk* as he imagines

himself "arm in arm with Balzac and Dumas" and suffering neither "scorn nor condescension" from the likes of Aristotle and Aurelius.[3] What was true for Du Bois has been likewise true for African American writers from Anna Julia Cooper to Ralph Ellison. Indeed, it is to oversimplify only a bit to say that the untenability of a literary color line drove such movements as the Harlem Renaissance. But if to insist on a manifold literary inheritance could count, for the likes of Du Bois and Ellison (who defiantly deemed Eliot, Malraux, Dostoevsky, and Faulkner his "literary" ancestors), as both a demonstration of the irrationality of segregation and a refutation of charges that black cultural expression was inferior to works produced by whites, what broader political work, in the postsegregation era, remained and remains to be done by black Americans through the writing and critiquing of literary fiction or perhaps through the writing of any fiction whatsoever?[4]

In the late 1980s, according to novelist and essayist Trey Ellis, the eclecticism of those younger blacks who could "admit liking both Jim and Toni Morrison" betokened "an open-ended New Black Aesthetic . . . that shamelessly borrows and reassembles across both race and class lines." In serving as the drum major of this new aesthetic, Ellis openly celebrates it as an indication of the substratum of the black middle class coming into self-consciousness. He writes:

> For the first time in our history we are producing a critical mass of college graduates who are children of college graduates themselves. Like most artistic booms, the NBA [New

Black Aesthetic] is a post-bourgeois movement driven by a second generation of middle class. Having scraped their way to relative wealth and, too often, crass materialism, our parents have freed (or compelled) us to bite those hands that fed us and sent us to college. We now feel secure enough to attend art school instead of medical school.[5]

In other words, these writers, artists, and their nonliterary peers were emerging as members of the rising professional managerial class for whom the doors to private schools at all levels of the educational system had been opened and, along with them, a concomitant bohemianism that allowed those who weren't ultimately to make their way as professional writers and artists to defer the moment when they succumbed to the yoke of necessity that would result, after all was said and done, in an MD, JD, PhD, or senior management position in an appropriately large corporate firm. And once they were safely ensconced in reasonably well-salaried positions, they could remain connected to the movement through their sensibilities, styles of consumption, and willingness to bankroll the artists and filmmakers who continued to produce the expressions that gave meaning to their patterns of life. All in all, depending on how one chose to look at it, this group could appear simultaneously as the culmination of the past or a break with it.

Adolph Reed, in analyzing black petit bourgeois fascination with Du Bois's turn-of-the-century notion of double consciousness, has laid out perhaps the most thoroughgoing analysis of this group, observing that the trope of ambivalence "is a key metaphor around which the stratum congeals as a distinct entity; it is a condensation symbol that mediates the movement from abstract statistical aggregate to self-conscious reference group." The métier of this stratum is self-expression, and its genre of choice is the memoir, which black writers, like their white, brown, and yellow counterparts, published with systematic regularity in the late 1980s and early 1990s: Michael Awkward, Stephen L. Carter, Lorene Cary, Henry Louis Gates Jr., Deborah McDowell, Leanita McClain, and Patricia Williams, to name a few, were among those contributing to this stream of self-reflection. And when they weren't tapping out official memoirs, the style and sensibility of the personal narrative infiltrated their fiction, their literary criticism, and their social analysis. The ambivalence expressed in and constitutive of these texts served these writers as "a marker of elevated status and an artifact of the racial burden borne uniquely by elite nonwhites" that could "express in the same instant celebration and complaint.[6]

Observing a decade earlier the harbinger of what Ellis would eventually declare a new movement in flower, Ralph Ellison writes of "a light-skinned, blue-eyed, Afro-American-featured individual who could have been taken for anything from a sun-tinged white Anglo-Saxon, an Egyptian, or a mixed-breed American Indian to a strayed member of certain tribes of Jews." What makes notable the appearance of this young man on "New York's Riverside Drive near 151st Street" is not merely his racial ambiguity but also the stylistic eclecticism and behavior accompanying it. His dress includes "black riding boots and fawn-colored riding breeches of English tailoring," a "leather riding crop," a "dashing dashiki," and a "black homburg hat" atop "his huge Afro-coiffed head." His emergence onto the scene at Riverside Drive from a Volkswagen Beetle is a choreographed spectacle that he himself documents with a "Japanese single-lens-reflex camera" before which he poses as if he were a model at a fashion shoot. For Ellison, the man's

> carefully stylized movements (especially his "pimp-limp" walk) marked him as a native of the U.S.A., a home-boy bent upon projecting and recording with native verve something of his complex sense of cultural identity. Clearly he had his own style, but if—as has been repeatedly argued—the style is the man, who on earth was this fellow? Viewed from a rigid ethnocultural perspective, neither his features nor his car nor his dress was of a whole. Yet he conducted himself with an obvious pride of person and of property, inviting all and sundry to admire and wonder in response to himself as his own sign and symbol, his own work of art.[7]

Of course, from the chic perspective of the New Black Aestheticians, the sartorial display of Ellison's multicultural messiah would be altogether passé. For them, "little, round glasses" could do the work of more garish props, while "kinte-cloth scarves" and "tiny, neat dreadlocks" replaced dashikis and large Afros.[8] But for Ellison and Ellis alike, the avatars of this unapologetic playing of the cultural "appropriation game" signaled the inadequacy of the Black Aesthetic sensibility that had emerged in the late 1960s and early 1970s as a means of understanding the cultural reality of what black Americans were experiencing at the moment.[9] Neither Ellison nor Ellis was ready to declare Black Nationalism entirely irrelevant. Ellison admits that for all his eclecticism, the man on Riverside Drive "may have been" a "militant black nationalist bent upon dramatizing his feelings of alienation,"[10] while in Ellis's view, "Nationalist pride continues to be one of the strongest forces in the black community and the New Black Aesthetic stems straight from that tradition. It is not an apolitical, art-for-art's-sake fantasy."[11] As Adolph Reed observes, Ellis "presents nationalism as the marker of black political authenticity," thus reducing it to a depoliticized icon. But an "iconic nationalism" is all that Ellis needs in order to underwrite the possibility that in the cultural free-for-all that constitutes this new moment, something persists (or should persist) to distinguish black expression from its white and ethnic counterparts, and, more importantly, to root these aesthetic practices, however tenuously, in the "black community."[12]

Unsurprisingly, the views of Ellison and Ellis are not entirely congruent. Buffeted by the storms of the Black Arts Movement, Ellison characteristically makes recourse to the "democratic ideal . . . of our unity-in-diversity, our oneness-in-manyness" to account for the apparently outlandish figure in his essay, whose "garments were, literally and figuratively, of many colors and cultures, his racial identity interwoven of many strands." Against a "nationalism" that rests on an insistence that the primary identification of black Americans lay in their African past, Ellison declares of his home-boy that

Whatever his politics, sources of income, hierarchal status and such, he revealed his essential "Americanness" in his free-wheeling assault upon traditional forms of the Western aesthetic. Whatever the identity he presumed to project, he was exercising an American freedom and was a product of the melting pot and the conscious or unconscious comedy it brews. Culturally he was an American joker. If his Afro and dashiki symbolized protest, his boots, camera, Volkswagen and homburg imposed certain qualifications upon that protest.[13]

For Ellis, by contrast, the Americanness of this new phenomenon fades to the background as a becalmed sea—in his words the "horse latitudes for mainstream culture"—against which the vitality and dynamism of the New Black Aesthetic stand out by contrast. Notwithstanding its promiscuity when it comes to finding sources for its work, this new aesthetic claimed to derive its distinctiveness—like Langston Hughes's Negro artist from the 1920s and Addison Gayle's Black Arts writer from the 1960s and 1970s—from being able to project as its primary audience only those who shared its sensibilities. So although its actual audience, as Reed points out, may have been predominantly white, its stance could be that of haughty self-regard.[14] The late-1980s cultural offerings of artists and performers like Whitney Houston and Lionel Ritchie serve as cautionary tales for failing to play to one's own crowd. For Ellis, the "two now-pop singers have transformed themselves into cultural-mulatto, assimilationist nightmares; neutered mutations instead of thriving hybrids. Trying to please both worlds instead of themselves, they end up truly pleasing neither."[15] Of course, Ellis's assessment of what truly pleases black and white audiences dances past the question of how to account for the fact that the songs for which he, respectively, disparages Houston and Ritchie were also chart-toppers, but his reticence on this point speaks volumes: It is only the taste of a select few that interests him.

It is not the case that the lives of Ellis and his peers are racism-free zones. Rather, some measure of racism is to be assumed. The key is, whenever these occasional reminders of American inequality put in an appearance, to meet them with nonchalance. As Ellis puts it, "For us racism is a hard little-changing constant that neither surprises nor enrages." More important was how much one could do despite racial prejudice. In Ellis's words, "We're not saying racism doesn't exist; we're just saying it's not an excuse." So one would be well advised to heed the example of filmmaker Robert Townsend, who, according to Ellis, "took the dominant culture's credit cards and clobbered it with a film."[16]

That the dominant culture doesn't appear to have been staggered by the blow of Townsend's auteurism is beside the point (admittedly an unnecessary cheap shot at Ellis, for whom the unfortunate coincidence of having a surname that truncates that of a more formidable predecessor is perhaps burden enough). Closer to the heart of the matter analytically is Ellis's unmistakable optimism about the prospects of this moment. No longer burdened by the sense that cultural avant-gardism is merely a thing of the past, Ellis can declare with playwright George Wolfe: "'This is an incredible time.' It has been over a year now that I don't envy any other age. I feel good."[17]

Sharing in this feel-good moment is the eponymous protagonist of Andrea Lee's 1984 novel *Sarah Phillips,* whose biogra-
phy echoes, with some differences, that of Lee herself as well
as that of Ellis. Although raised in "the hermetic world of the
old-fashioned black bourgeoisie," in contrast to Ellis's upbring-
ing "in the predominantly white, middle and working-class
suburbs around Ann Arbor, Michigan, and New Haven, Connecticut," Sarah Phillips partakes in Ellis's experience of being
part of "a generation of children educated in newly integrated
schools and impatient to escape the outworn rituals of their
parents."[18] Likewise, by the end of Lee's novel, albeit in a tone
more poignant than bombastic, Sarah Phillips locates herself,
hopefully, in the current of a new generation:

> I had a brief new impression: that the world was a place full
> of kids in transit, people like the jogger and Lucy Consalves
> and that punk from Linvilla, P.A., all of them, inexplicably,
> bound on excursions that might end up being glorious or
> stupid or violent, but that certainly moved in a direction away
> from anything they had ever known. I was one of them, and
> although I didn't know what direction I was heading in, and
> had only a faint idea yet of what I was leaving behind, the
> sense of being in motion was a thrill that made up for a lot.[19]

Phillips's "place full of kids in transit" is not constituted solely
of young blacks. It is, however, emblematized by a black "kid of
about seventeen or eighteen . . . jogging on the sand" of a Connecticut beach where one would not have expected him.[20] And
because it is a place that contains motion, its "inhabitants" can

find themselves at once dislocated and at home. The burden of this new aesthetic, which again is simultaneously cause for complaint and celebration, is that one can be black and be anywhere, and one can be anywhere and still be black.

Almost a decade after the publication of Ellis's manifesto, it is dislocation rather than at-homeness that predominates in Michael Thomas's *Man Gone Down,* whose nameless protagonist strives over the course of four days to salvage the fortunes of his interracial nuclear family. Living in New York but temporarily exiled from his wife and three young children who have returned to Massachusetts for the summer, Thomas's narrator is a troubled but multitalented man: an aspiring novelist, a carpenter, a poet, an ABD in English (with an unfinished dissertation titled "Eliot, Modernism, and Metaphysics"), a musician and songwriter, with a range of influences that include Bob Dylan, Ray Charles, Sly Stone, and Robert Johnson. His childhood was traumatic. Abused by both parents and sodomized at age 7 by an unknown man in the bathroom of the Brighton Boys Club, he is already an alcoholic before he reaches age 20. As an adult he loses, and is still mourning, a childhood best friend, who perished in the collapse of the World Trade Center. Yet in the years before the story begins, he has pulled himself together enough to have gotten married and fathered three children. His wife, Claire, is white, from a venerable Boston family, and the phenotypical variety displayed by his children externalizes the tensions and ambivalences he feels inside himself. His older son, Cecil, who prefers to be called simply, "C," is dark-skinned and for that reason has already been subjected to racist remarks by his private-school classmates, who have teased him for being "brown as poop." The younger son, Michael, who goes by the initial "X," looks just like his father except with skin so white he could pass. And then there is his little girl, who is never named but whose brown eyes suggest she is more like her older than her younger brother.

The problem for the protagonist at the beginning of the novel, which begins on the eve of his thirty-fifth birthday, is how, in four days, to raise $12,000 to pay private school tuition for his kids and the rent and security deposit on a new apartment. As Claire has told him, *"We need to make $140,000 a year."*[21] As part of this effort, he needs to find suitable employment and avoid the temptations to cheat on his wife that present themselves to him as he seeks to fulfill his quest. If the narrator's problem is to avoid sinking into insolvency and divorce, the problem the novel sets for itself is understanding why the protagonist's concerns, which one reviewer rightly describes as "bourgeois," should count as a matter for "the race."[22] Beyond the general regard we feel for another human being in dire circumstances, is there any reason we should hear in the troubled timbre of the novel's narrative voice either the collective desire of what Richard Wright in his time called 12 million (now roughly 36 million) black voices or the voice of Ellison's invisible narrator that somehow in its lower frequencies speaks for us all? If Thomas's man "goes down," then does it somehow count as a loss for all of us with brown skins?

The life itinerary of Thomas's man (which in many ways parallels that of his author) weaves him personally into iconic moments and processes that characterize post–Jim Crow America. He was among the black kids bused into Southie in 1970s Boston, and among those selected to attend white private schools and to be admitted to elite colleges. He has known prejudice of the upscale sort (the surprise of wealthy whites who stare at him when he queues up at the trendy "North African and Middle Eastern stores" because they lack the "imagination to understand that I like olive oil and the bargain prices on Bulgarian feta, too") and of the vulgar sort (being called a "nigger" as a kid, hearing his mother called "ugly" by a classmate, and being referred to as the "big nig" by a man at a carpentry job); he has known gentrification in Brooklyn through his interaction with "the neopioneers—a strange breed of professional liberal whites who'd rejected their suburban origins then rejected Manhattan's crush and bustle" by whom he gets "eyeballed like I don't belong."[23]

Mostly, he knows the sense of being a "social experiment," which is to say that he understands himself and his generational peers as test subjects whose responses will tell us whether or not the experiment in racial integration has any chance of working for black and white alike. From one angle, the results are not promising. He tells us that it is far from clear that racial integration of the sort he has known was the original point anyway. He repeats,

> It's a strange thing to go through life as a social experiment, especially when the ones who conceived the experiment, the visionaries with sight of the end, and with an understanding

of the means, are all gone. No more DuBois [*sic*]. No more
Locke. No more Gandhi. No more King. No more groovy
social theorists or hippies or activists or anthems.[24]

Or to put it more prosaically, with the struggles of the civil
rights era now in the rearview mirror of history, the policies and
programs resulting from that time seem, in the eyes of the narrator, to have gone awry. In the absence of a broad movement
for social justice, just how do the personal victories and defeats
of those with petit bourgeois aspirations matter in the broadest
sense? To compound matters, these individuals have now become parents and face the question of how their children will
cope with a world that still bedevils them. Reflecting on the trials awaiting his own mixed-race children as they begin their
schooling, the narrator worries that he and his wife have

thrown them into another mess, the social experiment
redux—an ahistorical one at that. Now, however, there is at
least one brown kid per class instead of per grade. It's another
disaster. Brown kids as cultural experiences for the white ones.
The teachers, the administrators, seem to believe that they
are all on equal ground, but if they'd stop and think for just a
moment, they'd realize that there is no shortage in experiencing the glory of white people in this country—this world.[25]

In other words, his children have been pitched headlong into a
world where diversity has become a compelling educational
interest, and their value to the institutions in which they find
themselves is that they embody and provide this needed asset.

The narrator's grievance with a social order structured to glorify whiteness despite its apparent openness to diversity reflects a strain of complaint among the members of this stratum that often cashes out as a desire to "recreate" the enclave of black mutual support that the segregation order supposedly allowed for—a desire that, as Reed points out, often gives way to "a nostalgic tale of decline from an organic golden age."[26] *Man Gone Down,* however, skirts the full undertow of nostalgia for community by, first, confining this sentiment to a longing for the visionary leadership once provided by the likes of King and Locke. Indeed, of the narrator's childhood friends, only Donovan (also known as "Shaky" or "Shake") is black, and the relationship between the two has been more contentious than supportive. To be sure, the "where-are-our-leaders?" complaint is a feature of the desire for the organic golden age, but here it is given just enough historical content to allow for an awareness that they were men of their times, not ours. Accordingly, part of the narrator's continual source of dissatisfaction with his life is that he was raised to believe that he and those like him were next in line to lead his people. In another passage, which serves as a refrain for portions of the text, he laments:

> *I was born a poor black boy of above-average intelligence and without physical deformity and therefore I was chosen to lead my people, but some shit happened on my road to glory and I kind of lost my way.*[27]

The cadence of the refrain recalls the openings of Frederick Douglass's *Narrative of the Life of Frederick Douglass,* Booker T. Washington's *Up from Slavery,* and even the parodic rejoinder to this tradition provided by Steve Martin's 1979 comic film *The Jerk,* in which in his opening monologue, the character Navin R. Johnson, a white man played by Martin, tells us, "I was born a poor black child"—the last suggesting that what was once experienced as tragedy can now only be reanimated as farce.[28] It is not that Thomas's narrator doesn't take seriously the charge to be a leader, but that he sees multiple possible flaws in the likelihood of its realization. For him it may be *"because I'd sobered up or because my mother had died or because the world had changed—or because of all those reasons. Or because somewhere along the way I had become just too damaged to be of any use to anyone."*[29] From suggesting that only the inebriated could invest in the vision of racial leadership to intimating that the problem lay solely in the individualized damage he suffered as a youth, Thomas's words place the dream of racial leadership out of the realm of realization.

And this is not the novel's first critical take on the idea. Earlier, when considering the modes of being available to black students at Harvard, the narrator reflects:

Ah, the promised few: what a horrible burden. There's a limited amount of space for people, any people, anywhere. And on the inside of any powerful institution, especially for people of color, that space gets smaller and stranger. Most white folks believe the reason you've come in is to lift up your people. But you can't bring your people inside, except compressed into a familiar story that's already been sanctioned. And you wouldn't be there in the first place unless you were a recognizable type: the novel savage, Uncle Tom, the Afro-Centric, the Oreo, the fool.[30]

The leadership model, Thomas suggests, is a flawed representational scheme in which certain individuals who can manifest only as familiar types are then projected as leaders for a collective that can also appear only as a type. Manifested in this way, racial leadership exists more for the convenience of the educational institution than for the welfare of those outside it.

Also undercutting the novel's investment in the leadership model is the narrator's awareness of the extent to which what he experiences as racial exclusion is also—perhaps even primarily—a matter of economic exclusion. Like others of this class stratum, he has no illusions that racism has disappeared. In analyzing his sense of alienation from his white liberal peers, he says, "I know most of them are racists." But he also notes that the reason for exclusion was not "purely race" because there "were other dark people who became a part of the *us,* people who, strangely enough, arrived on the scene at the tail end of the gentrification." Not surprisingly, given what we've come to know about the narrator, he feels no kinship with these new dark people, in large part because he knows that despite the various "subdivisions of the us" that created differences and affinities, "the only relevant divide was those who could afford to pay and those who could not." The narrator's quest during the four days narrated by the novel for an annual income of $140,000 (admittedly not extravagant for a New York family of five) is nonetheless to become one of those who could afford to pay. Accordingly, after noting that his wife, Claire, probably didn't realize "that when the revolution did come, it was coming for her and hers," he also acknowledges, "When the revolution comes, they might be coming for me, too."[31]

Yet, for all of its awareness of the flaws of group leadership, the novel can't quite let go of the idea that the fate of its narrator and the fate of his people are somehow intertwined. In the novel's last section, when it appears that everything may yet fall apart for the protagonist, the notion of group representation resurfaces with all the trappings of parody but in a manner that nonetheless defies you to take it as merely parodic. Invited by his friend Marco to a country club to play golf with a group of friends, the narrator approaches his first tee shot, not only worrying that because he hasn't played in over a year he might embarrass himself, but also apparently with the weight of history resting on his shoulders. Never mind that this is well into the Tiger Woods era, the narrator cannot help but feel that something more is at stake than a friendly game of golf. Seizing what he knows is the wrong club to hit off the tee, he wonders if he is "the youngest or the first, the largest, Black Irish Indian to play at The Country Club." In addition, one of the two boys caddying for the group is black, and as the narrator lines up his shot, he notes, "Even the black kid is watching, and I can't help but think he has something invested in this moment, too—from a perverse claim to caddy shack bragging rights to the complete emancipation of himself and his people." But before the reader can fully take in this dramatic and apparently unwarranted raising of the stakes of a friendly golf game, the narrator is already upping the rhetorical ante:

> And I know, as I look down the fairway one last time, that to them, if it is bad, my first swing will be my last—*the one*—no matter how well I play after. There can be no redemption, not for him, not for me, nor for those to whom—because of some treacherous failure or triumph of synapse or courage (whichever you believe in) the many thousands gone, here and yet to be—we are linked. And I hear them, be it by spirit, madness, or some ventriloquist's trick. I hear them pleading, exhorting me to hit the ball straight and long, just as I hear the founder rasping from his canvas on the great oak wall— *"Swing, nigger, swing!"*—and his brothers hissing in unison, *"Amen."* It's too much.[32]

As readers we want readily to agree that this *is* altogether too much and that whatever is going on here, "the people" are best left out of it. Certainly the idea that a black caddy might invest emotionally, and derive some vicarious thrill, from seeing a clearly out-of-place black man best a group of white country clubbers at what could be described as their own game is not merely plausible but likely. But to see much more here requires some suspension of disbelief. Nonetheless, larded into the passage are references to spirituals, *Invisible Man,* Booker T. Washington, and the sociological notion of "linked fate," coined by political scientist Michael Dawson. This last concept, which Dawson defines as a cross-class belief held by blacks "that their individual life chances are linked to the fate of the race," would seem to give empirical grounding for the idea that what is happening on the golf course somehow implicates us all.[33]

Whatever skepticism we feel about the import of the moment, the novel invests heavily in it. The narrator does, to his relief, hit the ball far and straight, and his emotional response is so strong that he must turn his back so that the others will not see he has begun to weep. Nonetheless when his friend Marco tries to catch up with him, the narrator feels an urge to tell him what has just happened: "I keep looking into his dark brown eyes, and I want to keep crying. I want to tell him why— *'My people were on that ball.'*"[34]

It is almost impossible to relate the narrator's words here without feeling their absurdity (and it is a testament to Thomas's skill as a writer that the scene works at all), but the rest of the golf game, on which the narrator's financial fate hangs like a thread because of the bets the men have made, during which he and the black caddy do bond, and during which, in a flashback, the trauma of the narrator's childhood rape is graphically narrated in full for the first time, seems to argue for emotional authenticity of the sentiment. For the narrator, his people—which is to say, all of us who are black—were indeed on that golf ball.

So, what are we to make of the return of the idea of race-group representation in such an incongruous setting in a novel that seems equally invested in questioning the very basis of the notion? Dawson's concept of linked fate perhaps provides a clue, but it may do so not quite in the way that Dawson intends. The first point to note in the novel's apparent reference to linked fate is that the narrator seems to have gotten it backwards. Dawson's concept holds that black individuals believe their life chances are "linked to those of blacks as group" and make their choices accordingly. Political choices are likely to be governed by the individual's estimation of what is likely to be good for the whole. In the scene on the golf course, however, it is blacks as group whose life chances are presented as dependent on the action of a single individual—and as a group they don't appear to have any choice in the matter. Their fate rises or falls with his. To be sure, the fear that the actions of a single individual will reflect badly on the group as a whole is a standard feature of the racial situation in the U.S. social order, where racial stereotypes still have currency. But the risk of racial embarrassment here is rather small, in good measure because, for all the narrator's insistence that his people are on the golf ball, they are not in any real sense "there." In Thomas's scene, then, the claim of linked fate goes one way and not the other. It is the narrator, not the people, who insists on the exemplary status of his situation.

Thomas's inverted account of linked fate does, however, square with Dawson's concept in one important way. Dawson notes that, according to his data, "the *more* education one had, the more likely one was to believe that blacks were economically subordinate to whites, and consequently, the more likely one was to believe one's fate was linked to that of the race."[35] That is, the idea of linked fate makes the most sense for a man with the educational background of Thomas's narrator. He is precisely the kind of man most invested in the idea that what happens to the race as a whole implicates him and that what he does implicates the race as a whole. In assessing Dawson's argument, Reed has suggested that the evidence indicating that "race consciousness, expressed as commitment to the racial agenda seemed to increase, not decline, with education and income" possibly says "more about the class basis of the 'linked-fate' agenda than about the persistence of an abstract group solidarity."[36] In other words, to return to the narrator of *Man Gone Down,* whether or not "his people" need him to hit the ball long and straight, the narrator needs to believe they do. He needs to believe, perhaps despite himself, that what he does matters to someone other than him and his immediate family. To put the matter in broader terms, the idea that sustains the possibility of an African American literature is a belief that the welfare of the race as a whole depends on the success of black writers and those who are depicted in their texts. And while the argument of the foregoing volume has attempted to reveal the crumbling scaffolding beneath this idea, the hyperbolic recrudescence of the belief in *Man Gone Down* also demonstrates why the idea of an African American literature persists: Those who write it, and those write about it, need it to distinguish the personal odysseys they undertake to reach personal success from similar endeavors by their white class peers.

It comes as no surprise, then, that like its object of study, contemporary African American literary history—again, often despite itself—succumbs to the temptation to shore up a specialized intellectual undertaking by insisting on its efficacy as a contribution to the race as a whole. A few examples may suffice to make this point. In the introductory paragraphs of an essay in *Early American Literature,* Joanna Brooks writes, "Thinking, talking, and writing about race in America means transacting in matters of life and death, confronting the human capacity for profound creativity and visionless abandonment."[37] The context for this remark is a roundtable convened by Sandra Gustafson to explore how, in the seventeenth and eighteenth centuries, "discriminatory laws, practices, and attitudes existed in relation to a more fluid concept of 'race' than the one that predominates today."[38] In other words, the roundtable participants were asked to consider just how early the conception of race as we currently understand it began to do its work of subordinating a section of the human population for the purpose of the extensive form of exploitation known as chattel slavery. At first glance this would appear to be a question of intrinsic interest, requiring no additional justification to warrant its pursuit. Part of knowing our world involves understanding how our contemporary societies resemble and differ from those that preceded them. But as one reads Brooks's framing of this debate, it becomes clear that much more is in play than dating as accurately as possible the "'terrible transformation' enacted in law, policy, and everyday social practice, [when] African-descended persons came to be racialized as a permanent laboring class." Given that even "after the legal abolition of slavery in some locales, African Americans as a group continued (and still continue) to experience legally sanctioned vulnerability to economic exploitation, political domination, personal violence, and other forms of physical and social death," it is the case for

Brooks that getting the story wrong possibly "diminishes or obscures [race's] deadly inflexible reality for millions of people of color."[39] Mindful that historical inquiry "offers no solutions to the historical atrocities we study," Brooks nonetheless insists that scholars consider such questions as "What responsibilities do we bear to historical and contemporary communities of color? Are we content to talk about race as an artifact, or do we read and write mindful of its intractable urgency?"[40] There is little mistaking the answers Brooks wants us to give: At the very least we bear some responsibility to contemporary communities of color, and we must, by all means, keep race's "intractable urgency" always in mind.

Likewise insistent that the study of race brings with it a considerable burden of political responsibility is John Ernest's *Chaotic Justice: Rethinking African American Literary History*. Posing as its guiding idea a question quite dear to my own study, Ernest asks, "What is African American about African American literature, and why should we identify this as a distinct tradition?"[41] To reach an answer, he ranges across nineteenth-century writing to demonstrate that race permeates the whole of American society, past and present, and that a proper approach to African American literature will reveal that what "is significant about this literature in terms of race is its representational and analytical sophistication, its presentation of not simply the most conspicuous or crafted accounts of the conscious experience of race but also the best maps into the chaotic terrain of racial history and experience."[42] African American literature is the study and contestation of what race had done and is still doing to people. For Ernest, African American literature, then, is virtually isomorphic with the African American community whose "most prominent characteristic" is the "blended self-consciousness and self-awareness that follows from the un-avoidable necessity of addressing issues of race, social justice, and cultural incoherence."[43]

As its title indicates, *Chaotic Justice* seeks to solve, simultaneously, several theoretical and political problems. Recognizing the difficulties of making all of the various uses of the terms "race" and "racism" cohere across the last two centuries, Ernest turns to chaos theory, which is "devoted to the patterns created by complex and seemingly irregular systems" to do the trick. Because, on Ernest's account, race "encompasses the complex processes by which individuals are positioned, both socially and geographically, sometimes delimiting and sometimes extending privileges, options, mobility, and ideological flexibility," it requires a theoretic approach that can track all of these permutations and yet contain them in an account that reaches up and down the social scale and across centuries. The imperative for this work is not merely historical because "race has everything to do with cultural practices and institutions that govern our interactions today, for conditions of the past do not change merely because new laws are passed or old ones are overturned." The study of African American literature leaves us, then, with one question: "In short will we draw from this chaotic literature to address injustice or avoid it?"[44] Of course, one doesn't have to ask where Ernest will come out on this.

Perhaps a little less politically ardent than the work of either Brooks or Ernest is Dickson Bruce's *The Origins of African*

American Literature, 1680–1865, which seeks to track the development of "an authoritative black persona and the emergence of a distinctive black perspective on events" in American letters.[45] Casting his gaze back into the seventeenth century, Bruce argues that this process requires looking across a broad range of texts and discourses, only some of them properly literary, to understand what contributed to the nurturance of early black writing and why black authorship was demanded. Central to Bruce's study are the social and political exigencies that attended the need to oppose slavery. Black voices in literature were called for and asserted themselves to take control of their own lives and change the social order. Once established, this voice continued through the era of emancipation and, according to Bruce, is likely to continue into the foreseeable future. He writes:

> The themes and images, the stances created in the context of the abolition movement, building on frameworks going back to the seventeenth century, were kept alive by African American writers for a long time. Revitalized by events, made relevant by circumstances, they have continued to shape American ideals, and American anxieties, down to our own time. Until the color line is truly abolished, if it ever is, they are likely to continue to shape American culture, and American consciousness, for some time to come.[46]

Once again we find, in the ongoing practice of social subordination on racial grounds, the guarantor of a distinctly African American literary presence.

One hesitates to fault these scholars at all for believing in the political efficacy of their work. When Ernest, at the conclusion of *Chaotic Justice,* declares, "I make no apologies for my belief that both historical and political agency are possible through literary scholarship," one doesn't even want him to do so.[47] Rather, what would be more to the point would be to ask for specification of the nature and type of political agency he believes to be possible through literary scholarship. To his credit, Ernest has a model in mind: "a project—one hopes a developing movement—initiated outside the academy, *The Covenant with Black America.*"[48]

The brainchild of radio personality Tavis Smiley, the Covenant has manifested as a best-selling 2006 book of the same name (which has been followed up with two additional books by Smiley), a Web site, a twenty-city national tour to promote discussions of the book, and apparently thousands of book parties that were held as part of Covenant Conversation and Celebration Weekend in late May 2006. The guiding assumption of the Covenant is the need for blacks collectively to organize for social change. According to the Web site:

> It is imperative that we take this opportunity to consider the issues of particular interest to African Americans and to establish a national plan of action to address them. No longer can we sit back and expect one political party, one segment of the population or one religious denomination to speak for us or to act on our behalf. It is our responsibility as an entire community to no longer be left behind politically, socially, or

economically and to bridge the economic and social divides ourselves, by encouraging a conversation and a commitment that will inevitably benefit all Americans.[49]

The issues identified in the Covenant include ten individual covenants addressing everything from health care and education to environmental justice and the digital divide. In finding the Covenant appealing, Ernest describes it as

> a contemporary example of the historical approach I found among nineteenth-century African American writers—an attempt to define the terms *and the application* of historical scholarship by focusing on clear problems, manifest examples of an incoherent and unjust social system, and communities defined by an uneasy relation between local contingencies and national and global ideologies.

Ernest adds that Smiley's project reminds him "very much of the attempts by nineteenth-century African American writers to assemble an imagined community . . . that could identify itself *as* a community only by discovering itself as a scattered people joined by a common historical condition and mission."[50]

Like many of his contemporary counterparts, Ernest is concerned with the plight of those black Americans who remain largely shut out of the opportunity to shape their lives as they see fit. It is more than understandable that these scholars, having devoted a great deal of study to the articulation of literature and politics and having seen black literature given pride of place in the fight against injustice in the past, would be inclined to believe it can or should bear the same obligation into the present. What such an expectation acknowledges but fails fully to account for, however, is that the factors that pushed literary and cultural expression to the apparent center of black politics were antidemocratic: Slavery until the latter half of the nineteenth century and disfranchisement at the turn of the century disqualified large sectors of the black population from political participation. The system of race-relations management and elite brokerage that Booker T. Washington largely invented at the dawn of the Jim Crow era rationalized this disfranchisement by giving credence to the idea that certain African American individuals and cadres by virtue of their achievements, expertise, and goodwill could direct and speak on behalf of the nation's black population.[51] Such was the context that gave rise to African American literature—one in which the black literary voice could count for so much because, in political terms, the voice of black people generally counted for so little. Although in the works of various black writers across this period the literary voice strived—and sometimes succeeded—in sounding tones that were broadly democratic, more often than not it projected its own concerns as those of the race's generally and sought to shape a vision of justice that harmonized with, rather than challenged, its view of the true and good. The ending of legalized segregation, however imperfect it has been in desegregating American society, could not but change this situation.

Admittedly, the desire for a contemporary African American literature stems in part from the correct assessment that our post–Jim Crow society remains a society of dramatic inequalities and that black Americans are disproportionately represented among those who lack adequate health care, incomes, and other goods necessary to live a life of fulfillment in the twenty-first century. In the face of such disparities it is difficult, especially if one is black, not to feel some special call to redress these problems. Indeed there is evidence to suggest that black graduates from elite colleges—the group responsible for much of the literature discussed in this conclusion—are significantly more likely than their white peers to participate in those activities that could be described as "giv[ing] back to their community."[52] Yet, however encouraging one might find this statistic to be, it is important to keep in mind that to acquiesce in the logic of "giving back" is to acquiesce in the idea that one's "community" might, justifiably, be neglected if its "exceptional" women and men refuse to detour from the more lucrative careers they might otherwise enjoy to commit themselves to service. In addition, as Raymond Williams has cautioned, although a commitment to service has undoubtedly "been the charter of many thousands of devoted lives" and provided opportunities for at least an equal number of the economically disenfranchised to better their situations, this commitment has also tended to set the stage for individual rather than systemic explanations and remedies.[53] Further, it is often the case that "those who are ruled by the idea of service are genuinely dismayed when the workers do not fully respond."[54] Not surprisingly, the language of the Covenant subtly but unmistakably places the blame for the current state of affairs substantially on alleged black American passivity ("No longer can we sit back and expect"), underwriting, despite itself, a view of current inequalities as deriving from collective black shortcomings. It is difficult to see how a contemporary literary culture built on, or endorsing, this model could avoid affirming this logic.

To be sure, there is nothing wrong with investing in the idea that the writing of literature and literary criticism and history might in some way promote social justice. Many writers and critics sit down before their keyboards with precisely such ends in view. Indeed the goal of this book is to produce greater clarity around an area of cultural activity with the hope of helping us understand better where we are and how we got here. But as was the case at the dawn of the Jim Crow era, the impulse to call upon men and women of letters to step into the vanguard of social justice movements is symptomatic of larger inequalities. And we should be mindful of the fact that now, as well as then, symptoms are rarely cures.

NOTES

INDEX

Notes

1. The scholars and writers who insist on orienting black
   literary practice of the past century around Africanist
   practices and beliefs or the traumas of the era of slavery
   are too numerous to allow me to mention them all here.
   Certainly, among cultural and literary histories that insist
   on African- or slavery-centered accounts of current black
   cultural practice, one can mention Henry Louis Gates Jr.,
   *The Signifying Monkey: A Theory of African-American Literary
   Criticism* (New York: Oxford University Press, 1988); Houston
   A. Baker Jr., *Blues, Ideology, and Afro-American Literature*
   (Chicago: University of Chicago Press, 1984); Sterling Stuckey,
   *Slave Culture: Nationalist Theory and the Foundations of Black
   America* (New York: Oxford University Press, 1988); Saidiya V.
   Hartman, *Scenes of Subjection: Terror, Slavery, and Self-Making
   in Nineteenth-Century America* (New York: Oxford University
   Press, 1997); Molefi Kete Asante, *Afrocentricity: The Theory of
   Social Change* (Chicago Heights, IL: African American Images,
   2003); and Sidney W. Mintz and Richard Price, *The Birth of*

African American Culture: An Anthropological Perspective
(Boston: Beacon Press, 1976). Of course, Toni Morrison's
Beloved (New York: Vintage, 2004) stands out as the novel
most associated with claims about the ongoing influence
of the horrors of slavery on the collective black psyche.

2. Andrea Lee, *Sarah Phillips* (Boston: Northeastern University
   Press, 1984), p. 63.

3. Henry Louis Gates Jr., *Colored People: A Memoir* (New York:
   Vintage, 1995); Clifton L. Taulbert, *Once Upon a Time When
   We Were Colored* (New York: Penguin, 1995).

4. To be sure, this brief list does not exhaust the terms employed
   in the history of race-group naming. I could add here as well
   "Aframerican" and "Afro-American" and no doubt several
   others.

5. Valerie Smith, foreword to Lee, *Sarah Phillips,* p. xi.

6. Danielle Allen, *Talking with Strangers: Anxieties of Citizenship
   since Brown v. Board of Education* (Chicago: University of Chicago
   Press, 2004), p. 7.

7. James Weldon Johnson, introduction to *Southern Road,*
   by Sterling A. Brown (New York: Harcourt, Brace, 1932),
   p. xiii.

8. To be sure, elsewhere Johnson observes, "The line of American Negro authors runs back for a hundred and fifty years,
   back to Phillis Wheatley, the poet." See "The Dilemma of the
   Negro Author," in *The New Negro: Readings on Race, Representation, and African American Culture, 1892–1938,* ed. Henry Louis
   Gates Jr. and Gene Andrew Jarrett (Princeton: Princeton
   University Press, 2007), p. 378. But even if Johnson means
   to insist that this writing somehow always constituted a
   literature, his repeated observations that acknowledgment

of this literature is a phenomenon of the early twentieth century indicates the retroactive nature of the enterprise.

9. Erich Auerbach, *Literary Language and Its Public in Late Latin Antiquity and in the Middle Ages,* trans. Ralph Manheim (Princeton: Princeton University Press, 1965), p. 6.

10. James Weldon Johnson, "The Dilemma of the Negro Author," in Gates and Jarrett, *The New Negro,* p. 382.

11. W. E. B. Du Bois, *The Souls of Black Folk,* in *Du Bois: Writings* (New York: Library of America, 1986), p. 547.

12. W. E. B Du Bois, "The Negro in Literature and Art," in *Du Bois: Writings,* p. 866.

13. Claude McKay, *A Long Way from Home,* ed. Gene Jarrett (New Brunswick, NJ: Rutgers University Press, 2007), pp. 27, 85.

14. Quoted in Arlene Elder, *The "Hindered Hand": Cultural Implications of Early African-American Fiction* (Westport, CT: Greenwood Press, 1978), p. 69.

15. W. E. B Du Bois, "Criteria of Negro Art," in *Du Bois: Writings,* pp. 1000, 1002.

16. Henry Louis Gates Jr., *Figures in Black: Words, Signs, and the "Racial" Self* (New York: Oxford University Press, 1987), p. 25.

17. Ibid., pp. 26, xxii.

18. Thomas Jefferson, *Notes on the State of Virginia: With Related Documents,* ed. David Waldstreicher (New York: Palgrave Macmillan, 2002), p. 178.

19. Elizabeth McHenry, *Forgotten Readers: Recovering the Lost History of African American Literary Societies* (Durham, NC: Duke University Press, 2002), pp. 57–83.

20. Jefferson, *Notes on the State of Virginia,* p. 179.

21. Gates, *Figures in Black,* p. 30.

22. Kenneth W. Warren, "The End(s) of African American Studies," *American Literary History* 12.3 (2000): 637–655.

23. W. E. B. Du Bois, *Dusk of Dawn: An Essay toward an Autobiography of a Race Concept,* in *Du Bois: Writings,* p. 551.

24. Ibid., p. 573.

25. Du Bois, *The Souls of Black Folk,* p. 371.

26. James Weldon Johnson, *The Autobiography of an Ex-Coloured Man* (New York: Vintage, 1989), p. 211.

27. Du Bois, "Criteria of Negro Art," p. 994.

28. Sutton E. Griggs, *Overshadowed: A Novel* (Nashville: Orion, 1901), pp. 67–68.

29. Ralph Ellison, "*An American Dilemma:* A Review," in *The Collected Essays of Ralph Ellison,* ed. John F. Callahan (New York: Modern Library, 1995), p. 339.

30. Richard Wright, *Black Boy (American Hunger),* in *Richard Wright: Later Works* (New York: Library of America, 1991), p. 37.

31. Ibid., pp. 259, 260–261.

32. Walter Benn Michaels, *Our America: Nativism, Modernism, and Pluralism* (Durham, NC: Duke University Press, 1995). See especially pp. 114–118.

33. George Schuyler, *Black No More* (Boston: Northeastern University Press, 1989), p. 40.

34. Ibid., p. 55.

35. Ibid., p. 89.

36. Jonathan Scott Holloway, *Confronting the Veil: Abram Harris Jr., E. Franklin Frazier, and Ralph Bunche, 1919–1941* (Raleigh: University of North Carolina Press, 2002), p. 2.

37. Ralph J. Bunche, *A World View of Race* (Washington, DC: The Associates in Negro Folk Education, 1936), pp. 23, 29.

38. Schuyler, *Black No More,* p. 178.

39. "Virginia Racial Integrity Act of 1924," September 19, 2009, http://www2.vcdh.virginia.edu/encounter/projects/monacans/ Contemporary_Monacans/racial.html (accessed September 29, 2009). Jeffrey B. Ferguson notes that Schuyler's characterization of Samuel Buggerie "alludes to a number of race pseudoscientists, especially Walter A. Plecker, the researcher most closely associated with a series of race integrity bills that passed the Virginia state legislature in the late 1920s and early 1930s." See *The Sage of Sugar Hill: George S. Schuyler and the Harlem Renaissance* (New Haven: Yale University Press, 2005), p. 239. The story of Plecker's role in both the Racial Integrity Act and the genealogical study is told in Jonathan Peter Spiro's *Defending the Master Race: Conservation, Eugenics and the Legacy of Madison Grant* (Burlington: University of Vermont Press, 2008). See especially pp. 252–258.

40. Schuyler, *Black No More,* p. 218.

41. Gene A. Jarrett, *Deans and Truants: Race and Realism in African American Literature* (Philadelphia: University of Pennsylvania Press, 2008), p. 115.

42. Ferguson, *The Sage of Sugar Hill,* p. 6.

43. Ibid., p. 217.

44. Ibid., pp. 219–223.

45. Schuyler, *Black No More,* pp. 87, 195.

46. Ibid., pp. 94–95.

47. Robin D. G. Kelley, *Race Rebels: Culture, Politics, and the Black Working Class* (New York: Free Press, 1994), p. 51.

48. Paul Gilroy, *The Black Atlantic* (Cambridge, MA: Harvard University Press, 1993), p. 36.

49. Schuyler, *Black No More,* pp. 201, 208.

2. PARTICULARITY AND THE PROBLEM OF INTERPRETATION

1. Blyden Jackson, "An Essay in Criticism," *Phylon* 11.4 (1950): 341–342.

2. Mozell C. Hill and M. Carl Holman, Preface, *Phylon* 11.4 (1950): 296.

3. Arna Bontemps, "Negro Poets, Then and Now," *Phylon* 11.4 (1950): 356.

4. W. E. B. Du Bois, *Dusk of Dawn: An Essay toward an Autobiography of a Race Concept,* in *Du Bois: Writings* (New York: Library of America, 1986), p. 780.

5. "Racial Segregation in Education: Black/White School Segregation 2000," http://www.umich.edu/~lawrace/schoolsegregation1.htm (accessed September 21, 2009).

6. William Graham Sumner, *Folkways: A Study of the Sociological Importance of Usages, Manners, Customs, Mores, and Morals* (New York: Dover, 1959), p. 77.

7. Du Bois, *Dusk of Dawn,* p. 679.

8. W. E. B. Du Bois, "Criteria of Negro Art," in *Du Bois: Writings,* p. 1000.

9. W. E. B. Du Bois, *Black Reconstruction in America, 1860–1880* (New York: Free Press, 1998), p. 725. Du Bois's purpose in this book was to expose and counter as propaganda the predominant histories of the Reconstruction era. See especially pp. 723–728.

10. W. E. B. Du Bois, *Dark Princess* (Jackson: University of Mississippi Press, 1995), p. 296.

11. Du Bois, *Dusk of Dawn,* p. 714.

12. W. E. B. Du Bois, "The Conversation of Races," in *Du Bois: Writings,* p. 825.

13. W. E. B. Du Bois, *The Souls of Black Folk,* in *Du Bois: Writings,* p. 492.

14. Du Bois, *Dusk of Dawn,* pp. 715, 787, 789, 788.

15. Judith Stein, "Defining the Race, 1890–1930," in *The Invention of Ethnicity,* ed. Werner Sollors (New York: Oxford University Press, 1989), p. 86.

16. W. E. B. Du Bois, "The Board of Directors on Segregation," in *Du Bois: Writings,* pp. 1252, 1253.

17. Du Bois, *Dusk of Dawn,* p. 789.

18. Noliwe Rooks, *White Money/Black Power: The Surprising History of African American Studies and the Crisis of Race in Higher Education* (New York: Beacon Press, 2007), p. 1.

19. The Editors, "Apology," *Phylon* 1.1 (1940): 4.

20. Thomas D. Jarrett, "Unfettered Creativity: A Note on the Negro Novelist's Coming of Age," *Phylon* 2.4 (1950): 313, 315.

21. Alain Locke, "Wisdom *de Profundis:* The Literature of the Negro, 1949," *Phylon* 11.1 (1950): 5.

22. Richard H. King, *Race, Culture, and the Intellectuals, 1940–1970* (Baltimore: Woodrow Wilson Center Press/Johns Hopkins University Press, 2004), pp. 2, 4.

23. Gunnar Myrdal, *An American Dilemma: The Negro Problem and Modern Democracy,* vol. 1 (New Brunswick, NJ: Transaction, 1995), p. lxxxiii. It was Myrdal's claim that "The Negro's entire life, and consequently, also his opinions on the Negro problem, are, in the main, to be considered as secondary reactions to more primary pressures from the dominant white majority" that led Ralph Ellison to remark with disdain, "But can a people . . . live and develop for over three hundred years simply by *reacting?*" See Ralph Ellison, *"An American Dilemma:* A Review," in *The Collected Essays of Ralph Ellison,* ed. John F. Callahan (New York: Modern Library, 1995), p. 339.

24. David Levering Lewis, *W. E. B. Du Bois, 1919–1963: The Fight for Equality and the American Century* (New York: Holt, 2001), p. 449; also see, King, *Race, Culture, and the Intellectuals,* p. 39.

25. Hill and Holman, Preface, 296.

26. Alain Locke, "Self-Criticism: The Third Dimension in Culture," *Phylon* 11.4 (1950): 391, 392, 393.

27. Charles S. Johnson, "The Negro Renaissance and Its Significance," in *The New Negro Thirty Years Afterward,* ed. Rayford W. Logan, Eugene C. Holmes, and G. Franklin Edwards (Washington, DC: Howard University Press, 1955), p. 88.

28. King, *Race, Culture, and the Intellectuals,* pp. 2, 8, 10.

29. Alain Locke, "The New Negro," in *The New Negro: Voices of the Harlem Renaissance,* ed. Alain Locke (New York: Athenaeum, 1992), p. 2.

30. Countee Cullen, "Heritage," in Locke, *The New Negro,* pp. 251, 252; Locke, "The Legacy of the Ancestral Arts," in Locke, *The New Negro,* p. 254.

31. Toomer, "Song of the Sun," in Locke, *The New Negro,* p. 137.

32. Melville J. Herskovits, "The Negro's Americanism," in Locke, *The New Negro,* p. 360. Herskovits was famously to reverse this interpretation sixteen years later when he published *The Myth of the Negro Past* (Boston: Beacon Press, 1958).

33. Locke, "The New Negro," p. 9.

34. Leslie Fiedler, *What Was Literature? Class, Culture, and Mass Society* (New York: Simon and Schuster, 1983).

35. Larry Neal, "The Black Writer's Role, II: Ellison's Zoot Suit," in *Visions of a Liberated Future* (New York: Thunder Mouth's Press, 1989), pp. 36, 44.

36. Wilson J. Moses, "Segregation, Nostalgia, and Black Authenticity," *American Literary History* 17.3 (2005): 634.

37. Adolph Reed Jr., *Stirrings in the Jug: Black Politics in the Post-Segregation Era* (Minneapolis: University of Minnesota Press, 1999), p. 11.

38. Ibid.

39. Blyden Jackson, "An Essay in Criticism," *Phylon* 11.4 (1950): 341–342.

40. Nathan Huggins, *The Harlem Renaissance* (New York: Oxford University Press, 1973), pp. 199–201.

41. Langston Hughes, "The Negro Artist and the Racial Mountain," in *African American Literary Theory,* ed. Winston Napier (New York: New York University Press, 2000), p. 30.

42. Arnold Rampersad, "Racial Doubt and Racial Shame in the Harlem Renaissance," in *Temples for Tomorrow: Looking Back at the Harlem Renaissance,* ed. Geneviève Fabre and Michel Feith (Bloomington: Indiana University Press, 2001), pp. 32–33.

43. Elizabeth Renker, *The Origins of American Literature Studies: An Institutional History* (New York: Cambridge University Press, 1977), p. 2.

44. Ernest Hemingway, *The Green Hills of Africa* (New York: Scribner, 1996), p. 22.

45. H. L. Mencken, "The Sahara of the Bozart," in H. L. Mencken, *The American Scene: A Reader,* ed. Huntington Cairns (New York: Alfred A. Knopf, 1977), pp. 157–168.

46. Ralph Ellison, "Twentieth-Century Fiction and the Black Mask of Humanity," in *Collected Essays,* pp. 82–83.

47. Herbert Hill, Introduction, in *Soon, One Morning: New Writing by American Negroes, 1940–1962,* ed. Herbert Hill (New York: Alfred A. Knopf, 1972), pp. 3, 18.

48. Addison Gayle Jr., "Perhaps Not So Soon One Morning," *Phylon* 29.4 (1968): 396.

49. Ibid.

50. Ibid., p. 397.

51. Addison Gayle, *Wayward Child: A Personal Odyssey* (New York: Anchor Press, 1977), p. 115.

52. Ibid., p. 402.

53. Allen B. Ballard, *The Education of Black Folk: The Afro-American Struggle for Knowledge in White America* (New York: Harper and Row, 1973), p. 66.

54. Ibid., p. 124.

55. Adrienne Rich, "Teaching Language in Open Admissions," in Rich, *On Lies, Secrets, and Silence: Selected Prose, 1966–1978* (New York: W. W. Norton, 1978), p. 57.

56. Rooks, *White Money/Black Power,* p. 77.

57. Robert Stepto, *From behind the Veil: A Study of Afro-American Narrative* (Urbana: University of Illinois Press, 1991).

3. THE FUTURE OF THE PAST

1. Walter Benjamin, "Theses on the Philosophy of History," in *Illuminations,* ed. Hannah Arendt (New York: Schocken Books, 1969), p. 255.

2. Ian Baucom, *Specters of the Atlantic: Finance Capital, Slavery, and the Philosophy of History* (Durham, NC: Duke University Press, 2005), pp. 62, 80.

3. Judith Stein, "'Of Mr. Booker T. Washington and Others': The Political Economy of Racism in the United States," in *Renewing Black Intellectual History: The Ideological and Material Foundations of African American Thought,* ed. Adolph Reed Jr. and Kenneth W. Warren (Denver, CO: Paradigm Publishers, 2010), p. 19.

4. Ibid.

5. Nikhil Singh, *Black Is a Country: Race and the Unfinished Struggle for Democracy* (Cambridge, MA: Harvard University Press, 2004), p. 12.

6. Stein, "'Of Mr. Booker T. Washington and Others,'" p. 19.

7. Singh, *Black Is a Country*, p. 224.

8. Tommie Shelby, *We Who Are Dark: The Philosophical Foundations of Black Solidarity* (Cambridge, MA: Harvard University Press, 2005), pp. 4, 255.

9. Singh, *Black Is a Country*, p. 11.

10. Ibid., p. 10.

11. *Grutter v. Bollinger,* 539 U.S. 306, Supreme Court of the United States, June 23, 2003, *Supreme Court Collection,* Legal Information Institute, Cornell University Law School, http://www.law.cornell.edu/supct/html/02-241.ZO.html (accessed October 1, 2009).

12. Singh, *Black Is a Country*, p. 218.

13. Ellen Messer-Davidow, "Manufacturing the Attack on Liberalized Higher Education," *Social Text* 36 (Autumn 1993): 40–80.

14. *Parents Involved in Community Schools v. Seattle School District No. 1,* 551 U.S. 701, Supreme Court of the United States, June 28, 2007 (Thomas, J., concurring), *Supreme Court Collection,* Legal Information Institute, Cornell University Law School, http://www.law.cornell.edu/supct/html/05-908.ZC.html (accessed October 1, 2009).

15. Ibid.

16. Singh, *Black Is a Country*, p. 43.

17. *Grutter v. Bollinger* (Thomas, J., dissenting)

18. *Parents Involved in Community Schools v. Seattle School District No. 1.*

19. Among these titles are Mary Dudziak, *Cold War Civil Rights: Race and the Image of American Democracy* (Princeton: Princeton

University Press, 2000) and Penny Von Eschen, *Race against Empire: Black Americans and Anticolonialism, 1937–1957* (Ithaca, NY: Cornell University Press, 1997).

20. Singh, *Black Is a Country*, pp. 71–72.

21. W. E. B. Du Bois, *Dusk of Dawn: An Essay toward an Autobiography of a Race Concept*, in *Du Bois: Writings* (New York: Library of America, 1986), pp. 639–640.

22. Ibid., p. 666.

23. Walter Benn Michaels, *The Shape of the Signifier: 1967 to the End of History* (Princeton: Princeton University Press, 2004), pp. 138–139.

24. Ibid., p. 135.

25. Toni Morrison, *Beloved* (New York: Vintage, 2004), pp. 43–44.

26. Michaels, *The Shape of the Signifier*, p. 137.

27. David Bradley, *The Chaneysville Incident* (New York: Harper-Perennial, 1990), p. 391.

28. Ibid., pp. 439, 440.

29. Ibid., p. 431.

30. Not all readers of the novel agree that John's final act is an act of suicide. See, for example, Missy Dehn Kubitschek, "'So You Want a History, Do You?' Epistemologies and 'The Chaneysville Incident,'" *Mississippi Quarterly* 49.4 (1996): 771, http://www.accessmylibrary.com/article-1G1-168292079/so-you-want-history.html (accessed October 5, 2009).

31. Bradley, *The Chaneysville Incident*, pp. 206, 207.

32. Ibid., p. 213.

33. Melville J. Herskovits, *The Myth of the Negro Past* (New York: Harper & Brothers, 1941), p. 143.

34. Bradley, *The Chaneysville Incident*, p. 212.

35. Michaels, *The Shape of the Signifier,* p. 131.

36. Fred D'Aguiar, *Feeding the Ghosts* (New York: Ecco Press, 2000), p. 127.

37. Ibid., p. 229.

38. Caryl Phillips, *Crossing the River* (New York: Vintage, 1997), pp. 1, 235–236.

39. Edward P. Jones, *The Known World* (New York: Harper, 2006), p. 384. Emphasis in original.

40. Ibid., p. 385. Emphasis in original.

41. Ibid., p. 386.

42. Ibid. Emphasis in original.

43. Michaels, *The Shape of the Signifier,* pp. 129–149.

44. William Dean Howells, "The Man of Letters as a Man of Business," Project Gutenberg EBook, http://www.gutenberg.org/etext/724 (accessed October 6, 2009). According to Howells, "I know very well that to the vast multitude of our fellow-workingmen we artists are the shadows of names, or not even the shadows. I like to look the facts in the face, for though their lineaments are often terrible, yet there is light nowhere else; and I will not pretend, in this light, that the masses care any more for us than we care for the masses, or so much. Nevertheless, and most distinctly, we are not of the classes. Except in our work, they have no use for us; if now and then they fancy qualifying their material splendor or their spiritual dulness with some artistic presence, the attempt is always a failure that bruises and abashes."

45. Langston Hughes, "The Negro Artist and the Racial Mountain," in *African American Literary Theory,* ed. Winston Napier (New York: New York University Press, 2000), p. 30.

46. Langston Hughes, *The Big Sea (An Autobiography)* (New York: Hill and Wang, 1993), p. 228.

47. I don't mean here to ignore the fact that at various points during their careers, writers like Hughes and McKay explicitly espoused a Marxist politics. Rather, I want to draw attention to the way that in Hughes's description the problem gets posed as that of relating the writer as writer to the everyday lives of those blacks for whom the reading of literature doesn't typically count as a self-defining activity.

48. Nick Chiles, "Their Eyes Were Reading Smut," Op-Ed, *New York Times* (January 4, 2006), http://www.nytimes.com/2006/01/04/opinion/04chiles.html?_r=2&scp=1&sq=nick%20chiles%20%20their%20eyes%20were%20reading%20smut&st=cse (accessed October 4, 2009).

49. William Dean Howells, *The Editor's Study,* ed. James W. Simpson (Troy, NY: Whitson Publishing Co., 1983), p. 41.

50. Chiles, "Their Eyes Were Reading Smut."

51. Gerald Early, "What Is African American Literature?" *eJournal USA,* February 5, 2009, http://www.america.gov/st/peopleplace-english/2009/February/20090210134821mlenuhret0.1840784.html (accessed October 6, 2009).

52. Ibid.

53. Ibid.

54. Ibid.

CONCLUSION

1. Michael Thomas, *Man Gone Down* (New York: Black Cat, 2007), p. 99 (the novel was awarded the 2009 Impac Dublin Award); W. E. B. Du Bois, *The Souls of Black Folk,* in *Du Bois: Writings* (New York: Library of America, 1986), p. 363.

2. Thomas, *Man Gone Down*, 107; Langston Hughes, *The Collected Poems of Langston Hughes*, ed. Arnold Rampersad and David Roesssel (New York: Knopf, 1994), p. 23. The relevant lines from "The Negro Speaks of Rivers" are:

> I built my hut near the Congo and it lulled me to sleep.
> I heard the singing of the Mississippi when Abe Lincoln
>   went down to New Orleans, and I've seen its muddy
>   bosom turn all golden in the sunset.

3. Du Bois, *The Souls of Black Folk*, p. 438.
4. Ralph Ellison, "The World and the Jug," in *The Collected Essays of Ralph Ellison*, ed. John F. Callahan (New York: Modern Library, 1995), p. 185.
5. Trey Ellis, "The New Black Aesthetic," *Callaloo* 17.38 (Winter 1989): 233, 234, 237.
6. Adolph Reed Jr., *W. E. B. Du Bois and American Political Thought: Fabianism and the Color Line* (New York: Oxford University Press, 1997), pp. 169, 171.
7. Ralph Ellison, "The Little Man at Chehaw Station," in *Collected Essays*, pp. 505, 506, 507.
8. Ellis, "The New Black Aesthetic," p. 240.
9. Ellison, "The Little Man at Chehaw Station," p. 511.
10. Ibid., p. 507.
11. Ellis, "The New Black Aesthetic," p. 239.
12. Reed, *W. E. B. Du Bois and American Political Thought*, p. 168.
13. Ellison, "The Litle Man at Chehaw Station," pp. 503, 507.
14. Reed, *W. E. B. Du Bois and American Political Thought*, p. 167.
15. Ellis, "The New Black Aesthetic," p. 242.
16. Ibid., pp. 239–240.
17. Ibid., p. 243.

18. Ibid.; Andrea Lee, *Sarah Phillips* (Boston: Northeastern University Press, 1984), p. 4.

19. Lee, *Sarah Phillips*, p. 117.

20. Ibid.

21. Thomas, *Man Gone Down*, p. 5.

22. Sarah Churchwell, "Bridges over Troubled Waters," *Guardian*, July 4, 2009, http://www.guardian.co.uk (accessed September 29, 2009).

23. Thomas, *Man Gone Down*, pp. 101, 121, 122.

24. Ibid., p. 99.

25. Ibid., p. 248.

26. Reed, *W. E. B. Du Bois and American Political Thought*, p. 174.

27. Thomas, *Man Gone Down*, p. 217. Emphasis in original.

28. *The Jerk*, imdb.com (accessed March 10, 2010).

29. Thomas, *Man Gone Down*, p. 216. Emphasis in original.

30. Ibid., p. 147.

31. Ibid., pp. 123, 122, 209, 211.

32. Ibid., pp. 365–366.

33. For the notion of linked fate, see Michael C. Dawson, *Black Visions: The Roots of Contemporary African-American Political Ideologies* (Chicago: University of Chicago Press, 2001), p. 11. Also see Dawson, *Behind the Mule: Race and Class in African-American Politics* (Princeton: Princeton University Press, 1994), pp. 75–76.

34. Thomas, *Man Gone Down*, p. 367.

35. Dawson, *Behind the Mule*, pp. 81–82.

36. Adolph Reed Jr., "The 'Color Line' Then and Now," in *Renewing Black Intellectual History*, ed. Adolph Reed Jr., Kenneth W. Warren, et al. (Boulder, CO: Paradigm Publishers, 2009), p. 286.

37. Joanna Brooks, "Working Definitions: Race, Ethnic Studies, and Early American Literature," *Early American Literature* 41.2 (2006): 314.

38. Sandra M. Gustafson, "Historicizing Race in Early American Studies: A Roundtable with Joanna Brooks, Philip Gould, and David Kazanjian," *Early American Literature* 41.2 (2006): 307.

39. Brooks, "Working Definitions," pp. 316, 317.

40. Ibid., p. 319.

41. John Ernest, *Chaotic Justice: Rethinking African American Literary History* (Chapel Hill: University of North Carolina Press, 2009), p. 2.

42. Ibid., p. 251.

43. Ibid., p. 59.

44. Ibid., pp. 36, 37, 43, 32.

45. Dickson D. Bruce Jr., *The Origins of African American Literature, 1680–1865* (Charlottesville: University of Virginia Press, 2001), p. xi.

46. Ibid., p. 314.

47. Ernest, *Chaotic Justice*, p. 252.

48. Ibid.

49. Covenant with Black America, http://www.covenantwith blackamerica.com (accessed March 10, 2010).

50. Ernest, *Chaotic Justice*, pp. 252, 253.

51. On Booker T. Washington's invention of race relations, see Michael Rudolph West, *The Education of Booker T. Washington: American Democracy and the Idea of Race Relations* (New York: Columbia University Press, 2006), pp. 15–18.

52. William G. Bowen, Martin A. Kurzweil, and Eugene M. Tobin, *Equity and Excellence in American Higher Education* (Charlottesville: University of Virginia Press, 2005), p. 129.

53. Raymond Williams, *Culture and Society: 1780–1950* (New York: Columbia University Press, 1983), pp. 329, 331.

54. Ibid., p. 330. Oprah Winfrey provides a striking example of the dismay that the well-intentioned devotee of service often feels when those who are the objects of her good intentions fail to respond properly. When asked why she chose to open an academy for girls in South Africa rather than in the United States, Winfrey replied: "I became so frustrated with visiting inner-city schools that I just stopped going. The sense that you need to learn just isn't there. . . . If you ask the kids what they want or need, they will say an iPod or some sneakers. In South Africa, they don't ask for money or toys. They ask for uniforms so they can go to school." Quoted in Allison Samuels, "Oprah Goes to School," *Newsweek,* January 8, 2007, http://www.newsweek.com/2007/01/07/oprah-goes-to-school .html (accessed May 1, 2010).

INDEX

Aaron, Daniel, 71
Abolition, 16–17, 83, 140
Adventures of Huckleberry Finn
  (Twain), 71
African American art, recognition
  of, as art, 13–14
African American literature:
  collective social and political
  relevance of, 110; defined, 141–142;
  desire for contemporary, 146–147;
  development of, 17, 18; as distinct
  entity, 2, 7, 8; efforts in, 6; Hill's
  assessment of, 73; as historical
  entity, 8–10; historicizing, 1–43,
  97; imperative to produce, 16;
  indexical view of, 10–11, 14;
  instrumental approach to, 11, 14;
  in Jim Crow era, 3, 10, 22–23,
  119–120; as marked by Middle
  Passage, 2; maturity in, 114; as
  modernist, 72; as postemancipation phenomenon, 1; as prospective, 42–43, 67–68; public of, 9;
  racist assumptions and criticism
  of, 15; as representational and

rhetorical strategy, 9; as response
  to legal fact of segregation, 42;
  success of, as political tool, 10;
  teaching of, on majority-white
  campuses, 76
African Americans: antebellum
  writing by, 7; disconnect between
  ordinary and intellectuals,
  109–110; eclecticism of those
  younger, 120; as favored term, 4;
  need of, to organize for social
  change, 144–145; passivity of, 148;
  vulnerability of, 140–141. *See also*
  Black
African American Studies, 53–54
African American writers: achievement of, 18; during antebellum
  period, 3, 7; narrative devices
  employed by, 33; from the 1920s, 7;
  projected future of, 46; shortcomings of, as noted by Jefferson,
  15–16
Allen, Danielle, 6
Ambivalance, 121–122
Amenia Conferences, 32

169